ONE ON ONE

DAVE BAPTISTE

ONE ON ONE

YOUR PERSONAL

FITNESS TRAINER

VERMILION

LONDON

To my mother for her kind prayers

First published 1992 by Vermilion
an imprint of Ebury Press
Random Century House
20 Vauxhall Bridge Road
London SW1V 2SA

Project editor: Cindy Richards
Editor: Felicity Jackson
Designer: Grahame Dudley
Photographer: Shona Wood

A catalogue record for this book is available from the British Library

ISBN 0-09-175432-1

Typeset in Linotron Gill by Textype Typesetters, Cambridge
Printed and bound in Great Britain by
Butler & Tanner, Frome and London

WARNING

Consult your doctor before embarking on any exercise programme. This
programme is intended for persons in good health.

TO PREGNANT WOMEN

This exercise programme is not suitable for women in the first or third
trimester of pregnancy.

CONTENTS

FOREWORD   7

INTRODUCTION   8

SECTION   1   WHY EXERCISE?   10

SECTION   2   CASE HISTORIES   14

SECTION   3   ON THE ROAD TO FITNESS   23

SECTION   4   WHY THE 20/20 PROGRAMME?   32

SECTION   5   THE 20/20 EXERCISES   37

SECTION   6   THE 20/20 PROGRAMMES   125

SECTION   7   THE 20/20 EATING PLAN   137

ACKNOWLEDGEMENTS   144

Fitness programmes require enthusiasm, but excess enthusiasm can all too often lead to injury.

I have known Dave Baptiste for some twelve years: as an international athlete he used to suffer his share of injuries, like most other young runners, and he used to be treated in my clinic at the Crystal Palace National Sports Centre. Unlike most runners, however, he took advantage of his experiences of injury, and learned from our injury prevention programmes.

I have worked with Dave on his One on One fitness programmes for several years. He takes exemplary care of his trainees and, because of this, they have been able to enjoy to the full the benefits and fun of regular fitness training.

With this book, you can share the exercises Dave has used to improve the shape, fitness and confidence of many famous people. As Dave has motivated them, so he will inspire you to ever greater efforts.

Use the book wisely: if you are unfit, go for an easy programme, and gradually progress to the harder routines. Obey the golden safety rules, and never exercise when you feel unwell or in pain . That way, you too can take advantage of Dave's help to become fitter and healthier in the quickest time possible.

Vivian Grisogono

Vivian Grisogono, Chartered Physiotherapist
Head of the Fitness and Rehabilitation Unit,
Royal Masonic Hospital, London

FOREWORD

· ·

In the summer of 1986 my doctor gave it to me straight: I had 70 per cent clogged arteries, functioning to only 30 per cent of their capacity. I had no choice but to undergo heart bypass surgery – and let me tell you that's not a pleasant experience. What I couldn't understand was with that condition how come I wasn't dead, or had at least suffered a massive heart attack! My doctor's answer was that because I had been looking after myself for the past 15 years, after a near-fatal car accident in 1973, my body was in very good condition.

I owe a lot of that fitness to Dave. I met him in a London gym and, although I had done a lot of jogging and played tennis and badminton regularly, I felt I needed something to tone my whole body up.

Training with Dave is fun and on those grey rainy mornings when it's freezing cold and you'd rather just go back to sleep, you know he's going to be there ringing the doorbell. And he doesn't give up, so you know you've no choice but to get up and face the world.

I just wish he'd written this book before so I could have saved all that money I spent out on individual training sessions (that's just a joke, Dave, honest). Seriously though, Dave's programmes are excellent and I should know – he's put me through enough pain to prove it.

Adam Faith

INTRODUCTION

• •

Dave Baptiste is one of an exclusive new breed of fitness consultants, the personal, or one-on-one, trainer, employed by models, actresses, pop stars and businessmen and women to go to their homes or offices and put them through their paces. Long known among the rich in Hollywood, the personal trainer is now catching on in this country, particularly with business people who work long hours and cannot attend keep fit classes, and those who know they are unfit but haven't got the will power or knowledge to train on their own.

As one of the country's top personal fitness trainers, 32-year-old Dave keeps such famous names as Paula Yates, Adam Faith, and Carol Decker of the pop group T'Pau in shape. A former 100 and 200 metre sprinter who represented Britain, he branched into personal training about seven years ago after working in various gyms and health clubs as a trainer.

Unlike other keep fit programmes, his one-on-one system is based on workouts which are personally designed to suit the individual needs and lifestyle of each client.

Now Dave has devised the 20/20 programme, an exercise plan you can do by yourself in your own home, which is guaranteed to get you in peak condition in just 20 days.

Designed specifically to give you all the benefits of a personal trainer in your own home, the basic programme consists of just 20 minutes of cross body training a day for 20 days – an amount of time that Dave believes can be spared from even the busiest lifestyle.

At the end of that time even the most unfit will be in better shape. Depending on your own personal fitness, you can then progress to the intermediate and more advanced exercise workouts. The programme is extremely flexible, enabling you to follow it at your own individual pace.

Exercising regularly takes a lot of self-discipline – most of us can come up with a long list of excuses as to why it should be put off until tomorrow.

INTRODUCTION

With Dave working alongside them, his clients don't have to worry about motivation, he's quite ruthless and there's no question of stopping because it's raining or any of the other feeble excuses people use on themselves.

Knowing that only the truly dedicated are motivated enough to continue exercising at home on a long-term basis, Dave has devised for the 20/20 programme exercises that don't allow you to get bored – there's plenty of variety, they require your complete concentration and so test you mentally, and, most important of all as far as he is concerned, they are fun to do.

In addition to exercise, Dave's fitness plans for his clients – many of whom want to shed some surplus pounds – always include advice on healthy eating. His 20/20 programme shows you how to adapt your eating habits to suit your lifestyle while still being able to eat your favourite foods, and includes ideas for 20 breakfasts, 20 lunches and 20 dinners to set you on the right path and prove that healthy food tastes great.

SECTION 1

WHY EXERCISE?

· ·

When you are fit and your body is in shape, you look good and feel good, and this in turn gives you confidence to face the world. I coach a lot of people and the one thing that stands out more than any other is how much more energetic they seem than people who don't exercise. I'm not building superstar athletes, my training is about making people see and realise their full potential. Raising energy levels and awareness of one's body is crucial to being successful in the long run.

Fitness is for life and not just for youth. One day in the hot and humid summer of 1976 I was buying a newspaper in Piccadilly Circus in London, when I saw a tall man coming towards me. He wasn't young but he was walking bolt upright and was immaculately dressed. Oblivious to the heat and the seething mass of people all around, he was turning heads young and old. I didn't recognise him, but the newspaper man did – it was Douglas Fairbanks Junior. This was the genuine article, a movie star from a golden era, looking fit and fantastic. The image of him has always stuck in my mind. Those who look good in later life don't possess any secret elixir of life – if you train well and eat healthily, there's no reason why your quality of life should deteriorate in any way.

Ask any five people you know why they train regularly and you'll probably get five different reasons. Write down your own reasons and stick them on the bathroom mirror. If you're looking for success, get your mirror involved. Remember the mirror never lies, so don't lie to yourself, get off the sofa, put the biscuits away and take a good long look at yourself and ask yourself the question, 'Am I in good shape?'. And if you're not, you know what to do, and the longer you leave it, the more difficult it is to get started.

I've seen plenty of people go through the pre-training ritual. They think about it for weeks, promising themselves that they are going to start soon. Then they need to buy new training gear and spend ages looking for just the right trainers and tracksuit. Once bought, these spend a week or so keeping the wardrobe warm; then they have to wait for the sun to shine before they can start training . . . until finally they can't put it off any longer and it's time for the first session.

It is all too easy to start a diet and exercise programme with great enthusiasm only to lose interest within a matter of days, and while we've all heard about the high that exercise can give you, less is known about the very real low that many women suffer when they're unhappy with their bodies and have tried unsuccessfully to exercise or diet. This low can lead to a feeling of apathy and depression if nothing is done about the situation.

This is where a realistic, total body approach comes in. The main advantage of the one-on-one system is that all the exercise programmes are tailored to the personal needs of you as an individual: you progress at a rate that suits your fitness level, so you never feel the exercises are too hard, and no matter how unfit you are to start with, you are guaranteed to see results quickly.

However, exercise alone is not enough – it's no good throwing yourself into training with weights, aerobics or jogging unless you look at other aspects of your life as well, namely your eating habits and mental attitude. It is no good going on a very strict diet if it is totally unrealistic for the lifestyle you have; you need a healthy diet that is tailored for your specific needs, and that you enjoy.

It is equally important that you enjoy your exercise programme. Those people with wonderful bodies that look good all the time have developed the link between mind and body. Think of it in these terms: what goes on in your mind directly influences your body, and vice versa. It's a unique relationship that you too can learn to control and direct.

YOUR BODY

Before starting, let's first take a look at your body, and in particular at your physical structure.

We are all born with a specific body type that we have to live with for the rest of our lives – whether we like it or not. There are three types, the ectomorph, the mesomorph and the endomorph, each with their own characteristics.

Ectomorphs tend to be tall and slim with little or no muscle definition. They have low body fat compared to the other body types and are normally quite flexible. They have the fastest metabolism of the three.

Mesomorphs are shorter than ectomorphs, with a more symmetrical body, slim waist, wider hips and broad shoulders. They have good muscles throughout the body but are not the most flexible visually, which can make them look heavy and slow. Their metabolic rate is average compared to the other two.

Endomorphs are medium height and usually possess a rounder, softer body shape than the other two. Their main characteristic is a high body fat content, particularly noticeable around the hips and thighs, and their metabolism is slower than the others.

The first thing to do is to recognise your own body type, as only then will you be able to adapt and enhance it, and then realise that trying to change one body type into another is not only frustrating, it's impossible. But don't despair – the 20/20 programme provides the right exercises to help you adapt and enhance the physical potential you were born with.

BODY IMAGE

We all carry a snapshot, a one-off visual image, of how we see ourselves, and sometimes this can be a real spur to nurturing confidence – overweight people, for instance, who imagine themselves to be slimmer than they really are carry and project themselves as being slimmer – to their advantage. However, if you have a poor picture of yourself it can lead to problems – women who suffer from poor body image tend to push themselves very hard in training and have bad food habits and sometimes eat for comfort.

Poor body image can often be traced back to childhood when other children's hurtful comments took root and resulted in a lack of self-esteem that lasts into adulthood. The best way to boost your self-esteem is to find some distraction that stretches your mental powers and so helps you become more creative. Don't believe all those magazines that promise an easy path to eternal beauty just by following their advice.

MAIN PROBLEM AREAS

Being overweight is one of the main reasons for people deciding to start some form of exercise programme. Women tend to gain weight on their hips and thighs, stomach, bottom and upper arms, and need exercises to tone up these areas. Men tend to get flabby chests and stomachs and need exercises designed to give them more definition and symmetry. The 20/20 programme has been designed more for women than men, but men can do the exercises as well.

SECTION 2

CASE HISTORIES

••••••••••••••••••••••••••

JOANNA

Joanna, a 30-year-old film director, typifies the new attitude to looking after your body. Film directing is not the healthiest of occupations; you're either working day and night for weeks on end on the set, or you spend a great deal of time waiting for the telephone to ring for your next project. Despite the lows when she hasn't been working, she still manages to keep herself motivated when it comes to her fitness and food and at five feet six inches, weighs around 9 stone.

When we first started training she had a good shape but poor muscle tone, and her cardiovascular system was quite bad. She requested a total body programme covering mobility, cardiovascular, strength and more defi-nition. During the next few weeks Joanna did a lot of travelling, which meant she had to do the training programme I had designed for her on her own and away from home. After two months she suddenly became much stronger and more flexible, but still no definition. After going through Joanna's diet I couldn't work out what was wrong until I discovered she was a secret chocaholic! If she was under stress or feeling low, she would have a couple of bars of chocolate, but the instant high she'd get from the sugar lasted just as long as it took to chew the last bar. It was followed by another low, this time because she felt guilty about letting herself down on the train-ing programme. The enormous guilt she would sometimes feel was making her very moody; she is, by her own admission obsessive, and this made it difficult to know exactly how to cope with the problem. What I had to show her was that the odd bar of chocolate wasn't going to do her any harm. So, one day I turned up at her flat for training as usual and after she'd worked well and trained hard, I told her how well she'd done. At the same time I was munching away on a bar of chocolate. I then threw another chocolate bar on her lap to see how she would react. She seemed shocked at first, then after a few moments took one bite at the chocolate and threw the rest away and started laughing. She could then face up to her chocolate problem and it became much easier to get to the real heart of the problem – simple nervous anxiety, nothing more. Eating chocolate for comfort is something a lot of people go through. Obviously some restraint is called for to prevent you from constantly giving in to the sweet desire every time a problem crops up. Joanna realises that she had no reason to feel guilty every time she ate chocolate. Different moods create different needs, and you should be able to eat whatever gets you through, whether it is ice cream, chocolate, biscuits, sweets etc. but eat it within reason, not to excess. Joanna still has the odd piece of chocolate, maybe once every couple of weeks, her training is very consistent and she works hard to keep her new 8 stone 5 pounds weight.

For Joanna, exercise became a way of making her feel good about herself. Her approach to her fitness and food were ideal, but body success doesn't rest solely on how defined your muscles are. Joanna's performance in training also hinged on whether or not she was relaxed that morning. I developed a sequence of special breathing exercises, (relaxation is just as much of a discipline as being fit) that Joanna incorporated into her training programme. Now whenever she is travelling and working, whether it is Los Angeles, Paris, Italy, she does her special breathing exercises which help relieve stress and give her a new mental edge.

She has developed into a natural athlete in my eyes, one who is more than capable of working up a sweat solo. She realised that being fit wasn't a three week wonder job but a careful day-to-day maintenance to keep her body the way she wanted it.

Joanna's schedule has become even more frantic now she's taken another step forward by becoming an independent film producer, which basically means more stress than ever. She's busy setting up the new project, but still manages to keep her training going, despite the long hours and countless meetings she has to attend. But to my mind, she's already faced her greatest challenge by coming to terms with her mind/body connection, and finding a balance between her career and her fitness.

RICHARD

Richard is a 45-year-old photographer. If there is a big party, film premier or Hollywood star in town, he's the man who'll get the picture. But there is a price to pay for capturing the big shot and while most of us are at home getting ready for bed, Richard is getting ready to do business. No two days are the same in Richard's hectic lifestyle, which made it extremely difficult to develop a training programme for him. In order to understand exactly the stresses and strains he was under, I spent a day as his 'assistant' in London and got a real taste of his lifestyle. The first thing I was struck by was the tremendous amount of travelling he does, rushing from here to there.

I soon realised that one thing he will never suffer from is hunger. It seems every function he attends has enough food to test the nerve and discipline of the fussiest of eaters, and most of the food I came across when I was with him should carry a government health warning. The trouble with all the constant rushing around is that it does tend to fire the taste buds and what's a grown man to do faced with all that food? Well, Richard got stuck in, not while I was with him I might add, but at five feet eleven inches tall and weighing in at a good 13 stone 4 pounds he'd obviously had one cream soufflé too many. Despite all the activity, there is also a great deal of waiting around and chatting; these are also social occasions where you catch up on the latest gossip with friends, and if you are not talking you're eating, if you are not eating you're talking.

Richard, by his own admission, had let himself go. But having spent time with him before we started training I was able to understand exactly how his mind and body were working. He was obviously worried that his weight was beginning to get out of control, so we tackled that problem first.

I asked him to make a list of the kinds of foods which were available at the various functions he attended, and I ticked off the good from the bad. Out went all the fancy dairy stuff, fried food, biscuits and sweets. In came salads, fish and fresh fruit. Richard doesn't drink, so alcohol wasn't an issue. I also introduced him to the idea of always carrying around a bag of fruit so that if he couldn't eat any of the food on offer he could always delve into his fruit bag. It also stopped him snacking on chocolate in between meals. We called it the 'Pap lunch'.

Having sorted out Richard's eating habits, I then addressed the problem of his physical condition which was basically awful. He had poor cardiovascular ability, his flexibility wasn't much to talk about either and, as for his strength, well remember, that's what assistants are for, carrying all the camera equipment. On the plus side, Richard had tremendous will-power – and once he'd made the decision to get himself into shape he was totally committed to it. For my part I agreed that he could phone me at any time and, if I was free, I would get there within 30 minutes. It was an unusual agreement but one which I didn't mind committing myself to because I knew how busy his schedule was. I also realised that once Richard began to see improvements in his body he would recognise the need to make proper regular times for his training. Gradually he began to get more confidence as first his weight, then his training began to improve. He lost 12 pounds in six weeks and then asked if I would teach him how to run!

Richard's improvement was quite staggering considering he was from a non-athletic background in a physically demanding job, making positive and decisive changes in his lifestyle and coming up winning. The task wasn't over once he'd lost the weight either, he found out that if getting there was hard, staying on top of it was even harder. Richard's determination to get his body together was a big factor in his success. Of course there were days when he needed encouragement and support, but there was no better boost for him than watching the inches disappear from his waistline. After 10 weeks he was able to dig out a pair of jeans which he hadn't worn since the 1970s! Everyone needs something to inspire them, whatever it takes, I'm behind them one hundred per cent. Richard has learnt all the training exercises and now has his own training down to a fine art even to the extent of making sure he works out in his hotel room when he's travelling.

ARABELLA

As many more women gain a high profile in the business and media community, their success or failure is put under the microscope and the pressures can be enormous, particularly in the City. Arabella is a 35-year-old merchant banker with a work and travel schedule which left me in awe when we first attempted to synchronize our diaries and arrange some training sessions.

At first glance she didn't look to have any fitness problems, especially at five feet six inches tall and an 8 stone 10 pounds figure that a lot of women would envy. We talked a lot about her work and the pressures involved, the travelling and entertaining. It was obvious that she was becoming concerned about her fitness and was prepared to do anything she could to make improvements. As she's normally the first in the office, it meant we had to train at five a.m! I was amazed at how alert and keen she managed to be at the crack of dawn.

Arabella's concern was justified, she struggled in the mobility department and had poor body strength. But what became apparent during our training mornings together was that she definitely needed to relax more than she realised. The actual physical release of exercise was what she needed. Tension in her neck and shoulders noticeably eased within the first eight to ten training sessions, and she examined her work schedule to see if she could possibly take some time off to recharge her body as she was aware that all was not well. The real danger was burn-out: heavy mental and physical exertion sustained over a period of time can have a debilitating effect on the natural recovery powers of the body. In Arabella's case a burn-out, if reached, could take weeks or even months to recover from.

Our training was often disrupted by her travelling, so I worked out a training programme that she could do even when she was away. The physical benefits of the exercise were obvious, but more importantly it enabled her to rid her body of all the tension and stress. After six weeks we had only managed to see each other for training sessions which barely took us into double figures, but on her return from a trip to the Far East, I noticed a marked improvement in her strength and flexibility, not easy areas to work on with her travel and work commitments. when it mattered most she still managed to get not only her fitness level up, but improve her weak areas. Arabella doesn't come from an exercise background and I know how hard she has worked. She also eats very well and is careful about her food which can be extremely difficult considering all her travel.

Slowly, but surely, her body has changed shape. She now looks leaner and more compact. She did have slightly arched shoulders through tension, but all that seems to have gone away. Once the awareness was total her results were dramatic and I'm happy in the knowledge that she has finally achieved the balance between work and fitness. Sometimes those five a.m.

starts can really be tough, but when someone like Arabella comes through it makes it all worthwhile.

CAROLINE

Caroline fast approaching 40, five feet six inches tall and weighing nearly 11 stone, was also fast approaching illness when she contacted me about a training programme. She runs her own company, which she started from scratch, and she works all the hours that she can physically pull out of herself. The last time she took part in any exercise was at school and since then she has, by her own admission, neglected the exercise part of her life. Meeting her for the first time, it became obvious that she was embarrassed about her appearance – being overweight when you are very active socially can cause a great deal of anguish.

Most of Caroline's problems are connected with food – at the slightest hint of pressure or tension she heads for the junk food! She is in that vicious circle, depressed about being overweight and overeating to help comfort her through that feeling of depression. Knowing she is extremely dedicated to her career, my first aim was to persuade her to show the same application to her food and training, which wasn't too difficult because she had obviously reached the point of no return and was determined to get herself together.

My first tactic was to hold her training sessions at her workplace. Caroline wasn't too keen on this and it took some persuading but it was essential to bring it out in the open so that she knew she had a problem and could then deal with it face on. We started training really slowly in order to build up her confidence and stretch her body into relaxation.

The turning point came with the loss of three pounds after three weeks. Confidence was all she really needed, and after seeing some results, she obviously started to feel much better about herself. The whole process of training became much easier and she was on her way.

JANE

These days, getting your body in the groove can be inspired by many things. For some people it can be the thought of a new shape, for most, though, it is just the desire to feel better in themselves day to day.

One day a record company called me and asked me to train one of their artists for the duration of her recording, and after for the album cover. Jane is 24 and a guitarist; her band have had great success. She was working on her third solo album and hoping for success with that.

I knew this was going to be fun. Being American, Jane had her own ideas about training, and besides music people tend to be difficult to work with. She is quite small, five feet four, and weighed just over 8 stone. She's a very good musician who enjoys what she does, but she felt she was under pressure from the record company to come up with the goods as far as album sales were concerned.

She needed me as coach and motivator, and we got on really well, until it came to what exercise was best for her. America is known as the home of the fitness boom, but the various ideas it has spawned aren't the be all and end all, and when Jane and I sat down and discussed various exercises she had to accept that I was the boss and believe in my method or we couldn't really get going. I explained I was always open to new ideas and any input from her which I thought we could incorporate into our programme we would use. Jane obviously didn't need to lose any weight but she wanted to get her behind really tight. Her heart and lungs were incredible for someone so small, she really liked to get the blood pumping through her body with dynamic enthusiasm. It was great, I actually trained with her on some days, which I don't normally do.

All the frustration of being cooped up in a studio all day came out in her workout, which was fine up to a point, but you cannot push the body to its maximum day in day out and expect it to respond. I work on the principle that if your muscles are tired, you do one of two things, you rest or you stretch. This is where Jane and I had a small disagreement, I could understand exactly how she was feeling, but a good stretching session can be just as beneficial in relieving tension and stress as working up a good sweat. After a few days when she was obviously not up to working out really hard, she began to understand that she could not continue to work at such an intense level when her body was tired. We could now concentrate on getting her body back into the groove and ready for the album cover.

We all enjoy doing our favourite exercises, it's the one's we need that turn us off. Jane has really good abdominal muscles but even the best set need constant maintenance to keep them looking good. She didn't like doing extra repetitions to keep her definition, so I had to keep reminding her about the album cover and how she'd be letting herself down if she didn't keep working up to form. Jane's album went ahead without too many hassles, and I was really keen to see how she looked in the outfit for the album cover and when I saw the test shots she looked great. She's back in Los Angeles now, preparing for the band's forthcoming world tour. I know she is still fired up and working on her body regularly. It should be interesting meeting up with her again to see if she has kept that body of hers in great shape.

LYN

Lyn is an attractive and elegant 40-year-old who could easily pass for 30. So what makes someone like her call me in to change her body? No great mystery, just a desire to nurture and improve what she was born with. At just over five feet six inches tall and weighing 9 stone 2 pounds, Lyn impressed me with her determination to learn and work at getting the body she wanted. With a full working day combining her talents as an interior designer and novel writer, she managed to find time to train no matter what problems arose during her working day. She was really interested in developing more definition and wasn't wild about aerobic or cardiovascular exercises.

The first time I trained with Lyn was a shock to my system, it was the first time I had ever been out-talked by one of my own pupils! Still, I managed to use Lyn's talking to gauge her recovery rate. At the end of a cardiovascular section I would wait until she started talking: that meant she was ready to change to leg exercises. I only wish everyone's recovery rate was as easy to assess.

Lyn wanted to improve her general fitness, lose some weight from around her hips, and improve her tummy ready for the summer. I soon discovered that the reason for this was in her wardrobes – one of the largest selections of designer clothes I'd come across in a long time! Clothes are a brilliant driving force in the search for the perfect body.

Lyn's one weakness and we all have them, turned out to be an addiction to peanuts. Okay, nuts aren't bad for you, but they are high in fat and vegetable oil, and the problem with nut eating is that you cannot resist them. When did you last buy a packet of peanuts and just eat a couple and put the rest away? So, ridding Lynn of her peanut addiction was quite a challenge for me. Luckily the memory of all those designer clothes provided me with a unique solution. We went through all her favourite fashion magazines and picked out some stunning pictures and stuck one on the fridge door and others on various food cupboards in the kitchen. While this technique may seem a little primitive, its success can't be argued with. If Lyn felt like having some peanuts, the pictures acted as a gentle hint not to eat a whole packet but just have a few. It worked, as gradually over the weeks she reduced her peanut intake to a bare minimum. This isn't unusual for people who I work with, a great deal of them eat very well, but we're only human and prone to weaknesses. In Lyn's case training isn't a real problem for her, her attitude is positive and direct, but because of her work she has to attend a great many social functions which test her discipline. Another way in which we dealt with snacking was by training at Lyn's danger hour between four and five o'clock. We got the routine very smooth and slick and I created an atmosphere in which Lyn could relax and have fun with the training sessions. She lost three pounds in four weeks which doesn't sound a lot, but weight loss is not a priority on my training programme. Losing three pounds without any real conscious effort to do so is more satisfying in the long run. Short-term weight loss is normally regained on conventional diet programmes which Lynn had tried in the past.

By concentrating her mind and body together toward the sole aim of toning up, her total body awareness keeps her discipline intact, and she's one of the few women I know who works out every day, alternating her sessions between stretching and light cardiovascular days.

Understanding how her body responds to good exercise and healthy eating has kept her in great shape, and if she ever falters, one visit to those designer wardrobes will be enough to bring her back in line!

SECTION 3

ON THE ROAD TO FITNESS

· ·

Measuring fitness through a single precise method is quite difficult as we are all different in both mind and body. I take into consideration all facets of a person's life, including their work, hobbies and general lifestyle. Physically, I look at their strength, aerobic/cardiovascular endurance and flexibility.

STRENGTH

All my exercises involve the use of only one weight . . . your body. Most people who weight train reach a point sooner or later when they realise that there is only so much they can lift. Exercises using your own body weight leave infinite room for improvement, and are safer and less time consuming than using weights.

AEROBIC/CARDIOVASCULAR ENDURANCE

Aerobic or cardiovascular endurance is the ability of the heart and lungs to convert oxygen into energy for the muscles. If you get out of breath walking up a flight of stairs, then you probably have a low aerobic capacity. Any exercise that increases your heartbeat and breathing rate for a sustained period is aerobic. Aerobic/cardiovascular exercises are the ones people find most difficult to persevere with, but don't get discouraged – you can and will improve your aerobic/cardiovascular endurance.

FLEXIBILITY

This is an aspect which is often neglected when people think about their fitness. I always try to impress on people that any improvement in flexibility equals increased range of body movement and a higher quality of exercise.

HOW ACTIVE IS YOUR DAILY LIFESTYLE?

With the advent of a single piece of technology, the computer, many people's lives have been transformed and they now spend a great deal of time sitting looking at a screen. Even if you don't work in an office or have a home computer, compare the amount of time you spend sitting to the time spent exercising in one week – the discrepancy should frighten you into some positive action. Remember that almost any physical activity is better than sitting in front of the TV eating chocolate or pizza!

HOW FIT ARE YOU?

To help you find which parts of your body, and your eating habits, need the most drastic attention. I have compiled the following questionnaire. Answer all the questions in the different sections and then turn to page 29 to find out your score and see how fit you are. Your score will help determine whether you start the 20/20 programme at the beginner's level or a more advanced level.

FITNESS ASSESSMENT QUESTIONNAIRE

YOUR BODY

1 ARE YOU OVERWEIGHT?

A. *YES* ☐
B. *NO* ☐

2 HOW WOULD YOU RATE YOUR FLEXIBILITY?

A. *POOR* ☐
B. *EXCELLENT* ☐
C. *GOOD* ☐

3 HOW MUCH TIME DO YOU SPEND EXERCISING EACH WEEK?

A. *5 HOURS PLUS* ☐
B. *3 HOURS* ☐
C. *1 HOUR OR LESS* ☐

4 WHICH OF THESE SPORTS DO YOU REGULARLY TAKE PART IN?

A. *WEIGHT TRAINING* ☐
B. *JOGGING* ☐
C. *AEROBICS* ☐
D. *YOGA* ☐

5 DOES GOING UP A FLIGHT OF STAIRS LEAVE YOU BREATHLESS?

A. *YES* ☐
B. *NO* ☐

6 HOW WOULD YOU RATE THE CONDITION OF YOUR STOMACH/ABDOMINAL MUSCLES?

A. *WEAK* ☐

B. *STRONG* ☐

C. *AWFUL* ☐

STRESS LEVELS
7 DO YOU SMOKE?

A. *YES* ☐

B. *NO* ☐

8 HOW WOULD YOU DESCRIBE YOUR SLEEP?

A. *RESTFUL* ☐

B. *RESTLESS* ☐

9 HOW MANY DAYS OFF SICK DO YOU TAKE FROM WORK EACH YEAR?

A. *16 PLUS* ☐

B. *7* ☐

C. *NONE* ☐

10 HOW DO YOU SPEND THE MAJORITY OF YOUR RELAXATION TIME?

A. *WATCHING TV* ☐

B. *PLAYING SOME SORT OF SPORT* ☐

C. *GOING TO PUBS AND RESTAURANTS* ☐

11 HOW DO YOU TRAVEL TO WORK?

A. *IN A CAR* ☐

B. *BY PUBLIC TRANSPORT* ☐

C. *ON A BICYCLE* ☐

D. *ON FOOT* ☐

ON THE ROAD TO FITNESS

12 DO YOU WAKE UP AT NIGHT AND START WORRYING ABOUT WORK?

A. OFTEN ☐
B. NEVER ☐
C. OCCASIONALLY ☐

13 WHAT ARE YOU LIKE AT ORGANISING YOUR WORK/DOMESTIC SCHEDULE?

A. GOOD ☐
B. BAD ☐

Your Food
14 DO YOU EAT FRIED FOOD?

A. YES ☐
B. NO ☐

15 DO YOU EAT BETWEEN MEALS?

A. SOMETIMES ☐
B. NEVER ☐
C. CONSTANTLY ☐

16 WHEN DO YOU HAVE YOUR EVENING MEAL?

A. 6.00PM ☐
B. 7.00PM ☐
C. AFTER 8.00PM ☐

17 IF YOU SAW A FOOD CONTAINED AN E-NUMBER ADDITIVE IN ITS LIST OF INGREDIENTS, WOULD YOU:

A. AVOID IT LIKE THE PLAGUE ☐
B. EAT IT ANYWAY BECAUSE YOU DON'T KNOW WHAT E-NUMBERS ARE? ☐

**18 HOW OFTEN DO YOU EAT
FRESH FRUIT OR VEGETABLES?**

A. *EVERYDAY* ☐

B. *2 OR 3 TIMES A WEEK* ☐

C. *ONCE EVERY 2 WEEKS* ☐

**19 ARE YOU CONTINUOUSLY
TRYING TO LOSE WEIGHT?**

A. *YES* ☐

B. *NO* ☐

C. *PERIODICALLY* ☐

20 DO YOU NEED TO PUT WEIGHT ON?

A. *YES* ☐

B. *NO* ☐

BODY AWARENESS

21 WHERE ARE YOUR QUADRICEPS?

A. *BELOW THE KNEE* ☐

B. *FRONT OF THE THIGH* ☐

C. *BACK OF THE THIGH* ☐

22 WHERE ARE YOUR HAMSTRINGS?

A. *BACK OF THE THIGH* ☐

B. *BEHIND THE KNEE* ☐

C. *IN THE LOWER BACK* ☐

23 WHERE ARE YOUR OBLIQUES?

A. *ON TOP OF YOUR SHOULDERS* ☐

B. *ON THE SIDE OF THE KNEE* ☐

C. *ON THE SIDE OF YOUR BODY, ABOVE THE
WAIST* ☐

**24 ARE YOU CONSCIOUS OF THE WAY
YOU WALK AND MOVE AROUND?**

A. *NOT IN THE SLIGHTEST* ☐

B. *YES, YOU'RE ALWAYS AWARE OF YOUR POSTURE* ☐

25 WHICH WORKS YOUR BODY THE HARDEST?

A. *CROSS-COUNTRY SKIING* ☐
B. *CROSS-COUNTRY RUNNING* ☐
C. *AEROBICS* ☐

26 DO YOU EVER LOOK AT YOURSELF NAKED IN THE MIRROR?

A. *YES* ☐
B. *NO* ☐

SCORE AND ASSESSMENT

YOUR BODY

1 A–0, B–5
2 A–0, B–5, C–3
3 A–5, B–3, C–1
4 A–2, B–2, C–3, D–4
5 A–0, B–5
6 A–1, B–4, C–0

STRESS LEVELS

7 A–0, B–5
8 A–4, B–2
9 A–0, B–2, C–5
10 A–2, B–5, C–0
11 A–0, B–2, C–4, D–4
12 A–0, B–5, C–3
13 A–5, B–1

YOUR FOOD

14 A–0, B–5
15 A–2, B–5, C–0
16 A–5, B–3, C–0
17 A–5, B–0
18 A–5, B–2, C–0
19 A–0, B–3, C–1
20 A–3, B–5

BODY AWARENESS

21 A–0, B–5, C–0
22 A–5, B–0, C–0
23 A–0, B–0, C–5
24 A–0, B–5
25 A–5, B–0, C–0
26 A–5, B–0

90 or over

You're in good shape, but may need to mix your training routine especially if you participate in a sport which uses a specific area of your body. For instance, if you do a lot of running your lower body may be in good shape but what about the rest of you? The great advantage of the 20/20 programme is that it exercises the whole body. I would suggest you start with the 20/20 Intermediate Programme (page 133) but remember to take it easy to begin with and then try the 20/20 Advanced Programme (page 135).

40–60

You talk a good fight but now get working! Basically you're not in bad shape. You may have done regular exercise in the past and only recently become a couch potato? Don't despair, start with the beginners' programme (page 131) and if you feel comfortable doing the exercises after the 20 days then move onto the 20/20 Intermediate Programme.

20 or less

Lucky you bought the book! Seriously though, you are in need of the 20/20 programme. Start with the beginners' programme (page 131) but take it very gently. The first week will be the toughest but after that, once you start to feel the benefits, it'll get easier. Trust me.

TIME PLANNING

Once you decide to start a keep fit programme, you must make time for it otherwise you will never be successful. A problem I often came across in my early days as a personal trainer was clients cancelling sessions because they didn't have time. Fortunately this changed as people realised how important it was to put time aside each day for exercise.

You need to be equally disciplined at home and make sure you set aside time. Think of the time you spend watching TV for instance, and, if necessary, reorganise your life a little and cut down on activities that are not absolutely essential. If you're really concerned about the way your body looks and feels, you will make time for your training – it's all a matter of getting your priorities right. Remember, with this programme you need only 20 minutes a day. So be selfish, make time to get your body in shape.

IMPATIENCE

Some people want to run before they can walk, others want to see results yesterday! What you must understand is that the first effect of getting in shape is likely to be a mental one. The more you exercise, the more confident you feel about your body. As for physical differences, they really depend on your level of fitness at the beginning. I have known women see noticeable changes after two weeks while others have had to wait for four.

The important thing is to make sure you don't try too much too soon. This normally happens with people who were in good shape then, for one reason or another, got out of shape and are now yearning to return to their former glory. You may find it hard to believe that you would ever get yourself in this position, but overtraining is becoming an increasingly common problem, keeping physiotherapists and osteopaths busy treating people who have pushed themselves too hard. If you think you will never reach that extreme that's good, but lack of any physical changes can be frustrating and drive you back to your previous bad habits. Be patient and remember that your body will react gradually to your new exercise programme.

Quite apart from your appearance, changes can manifest themselves in a variety of other ways. You may find that your energy levels rise and that you sleep better at night. These things are just as important, as they improve the quality of your daily life.

SECTION 4

WHY THE 20/20 PROGRAMME?

• •

The choice of fitness methods has never been greater, but multiple choice doesn't necessarily mean a higher quality of instruction or of method. You've all heard of 'going for the burn'. Well, countless numbers of injuries later, that's gone. Now we have low impact exercise to protect the body from constant pounding.

I didn't want to design anything that wouldn't work or would put a strain on the body, so I spent days working with physiotherapist Vivian Grisogono, who has had years of experience working with both world class athletes and ordinary people. We went over each exercise individually, then tested them on volunteers who had never trained before, measuring their progress over days, weeks and months.

Most people think of exercise classes as something painful, boring and expensive, and imagine that everyone else in the class will be younger, slimmer, fitter and more glamorous than they are.

With the 20/20 programme you don't have to subject yourself to the embarrassment of being in a class full of preening bodies while you cower at the back trying to hide and avoiding eye contact with the mirror. You can change your body – from weakness to strength – in the privacy of your own home. You will learn to feel good about yourself and not to be self-conscious about your body. It doesn't have to be painful and you can actually enjoy training, either by yourself or with a friend. The exercise programmes I have designed are varied and interesting enough to prevent you getting bored.

The 20/20 programme is designed to help you get the most out of life. More than just an exercise programme, it will help your body rise above the demands put upon it in everyday situations. The first spark in your decision to get into serious shape will come from the mind, when you suddenly get a mental picture of how you would like to look. That's when you need a plan or strategy, and that's what the 20/20 programme is.

CROSS BODY TRAINING

It provides a simple, but more comprehensive approach to how you should plan and think about training your body. It is a unique cross body training programme – all the exercise plans divide the body into sections, and these are worked intensely one at a time for a few minutes. But the beauty of the exercises is that while working one section of your body intensely you are still working other parts. For instance you can be doing upper body exercises and they will be toning up your stomach muscles at the same time.

Technology is a fine thing and it has pushed the fitness world into new dimensions but, while I'm all for change, an increasing number of people come to me after they have been frightened off by the sheer array of hardware around. I think to abandon one's thought processes and let a machine do all the thinking for you when you are training is uninspiring. I'm not saying you should never use machines, but I don't think weight machines, for instance, work for long-term body development, and people often complain that the routines become very stale and boring.

I really want people to think for themselves and to learn and understand what they're doing with their bodies; to be able to see, hear and feel movement as never before. I've always believed in keeping my training structure very easy to understand and easy to perform. Obviously some of the movements are harder than others, but purposefully so, for the performing of a movement involving a degree of skill is essential in developing confidence while exercising.

The 20/20 programme is the culmination of years of work and studying, but its core is its simplicity. I have developed a training programme that holds the concentration, provides quality exercises that get results, and is fun at the same time. The beauty of the programme is that you can work at your own pace whether you are a beginner or have worked out before.

The basic programme (page 131) is aimed at beginners and involves 20 minutes exercising a day for 20 days. The 20 minutes are divided into five-minute sections of stretching and exercising different parts of the body. The programme aims to cover a four-week period, allowing two days off in each week.

The intermediate programme (page 133) is more intense and for this reason is 20 minutes every other day. The exercises are harder as the number of repetitions increases. By the time you have completed the intermediate programme, you should be fit enough to mix and match the exercises to suit yourself, depending on which parts of the body you particularly want to exercise, or you can follow the suggested advanced programme shown on page 135. Your achievement will largely depend on how you incorporate the 20/20 programme into your everyday activity. Your body will respond to the training given, your perseverance and belief in your own ability. Total commitment equals total results.

VARIETY

Making sure there was plenty of variety in the exercises was an important issue in designing the programme: after all, there's nothing more uninspiring than performing the same set of exercises over and over again, and I've avoided this by working different parts of the body day by day. I remember in the past how I disliked the repetition of running round a track, but it was a means to an end, and the end in that case was winning races. Here, the aim is simply to improve your quality of life by attaining a previously unattainable level of fitness.

The length of the workouts was another vital factor in designing the programme as I needed to be sure I could hold someone's attention for the length of the exercises. The final choice of these time periods was decided by how much time one would need to fit in all the exercises i.e. the shortest time for someone to work out and get all the necessary requirements for their body.

If exercises don't keep your interest and excitement levels high, it isn't long before you lose the impetus and enthusiasm to train, but the moment you start seeing changes in your body and you genuinely feel you are making progress, training starts to be easier – there's no better motivation than seeing the stomach starting to flatten and the sagging behind beginning to tighten. Even if you have a down day, try and do a little exercise. Psychologically, it is always more beneficial to do a little exercise at your own pace than none at all even if it is just light stretching. If you can exercise a little on a down day, you will appreciate the up day even more.

Each exercise is explained – how it works and why you're doing it. You have to be able to connect a particular exercise with a specific body area. It's not just a case of exercising the body and switching off the mind.

The programme sets out to provide you with a much greater range than ever before of energy-efficient exercises, so that you can concentrate on a particular body area without worry that you are neglecting other areas. Let's say you want more from your cardiovascular muscles, but you don't want to do any exercise standing up. Well, the side swing (page 78) – one of my favourite movements – is ideal as you work the upper body, arms, stomach and legs at the same time as the heart.

Like all my moves, it doesn't involve any weights. I have nothing against weights but I believe that unless you can carry your own body weight without any tension or strain, there isn't any real point in using them. I meet a lot of men who do weight training to improve their physique, and I once asked someone who weight trained three or four times a week, with a body similar to mine, how many press-ups he could do without stopping – he did 50. I managed to do 100. The next test was chin-ups on a high bar, and I did 35 and he only did 15. If it had been a contest of weight lifting, he would probably have won, but it's a bit like the hare and the tortoise – his weight training will only take him so far, whereas my programme will always help me to keep a good body strength, definition and a level of flexibility he would be struggling to achieve. Also, with weight training, once you get to a certain point all that's left is the prospect of trying to lift heavier weights. Whereas with my programme, the challenge when performing exercises using your own body weight is always there, and you can never get bored with them because of the daily change of exercises.

VISUALISATION

Some people suffer from a lack of confidence brought about by the belief that there are things they simply cannot do. Visualisation is a technique which I use to help them overcome self-doubt. It's very simple and straight-forward and you can easily do it at home while you are exercising. For example, in the case of a woman who wants her bottom a bit tighter, I suggest she forms a picture of herself doing exercises on a beach, with the sun and the sea, in a swimsuit! I always put the weaker link last in line when visualising, so the positive thoughts can overcome the negative ones. This is just one way of using the mind for inspiration.

Colour coding is another way of using the mind. Different colours bring about different moods and by wearing a colour pleasing to your eye you create a happy mood to work in. Using colour coding, you simply associate how you're feeling with a colour relating to that mood. All you need is to focus on the colour for just a few seconds before exercising. Summoning up extra strength from the mind takes time to master, just as it takes time to get your body into shape. With increased vitality, you'll develop your own methods of inspiring yourself, particularly on those days when you don't really feel like exercising.

The human brain is probably the most underrated aspect of fitness that there is, so don't underestimate the power of the mind/body connection. Every time you exercise, your emotional state can take you up or down. In the beginning it's easy to feel up – you've started exercising and you feel good about yourself. However, once you begin to achieve results, maintaining progress requires more than just working out – you need a challenging fitness programme, and that's where the 20/20 programme will help you by providing a regular, precise and exciting fitness plan. Now you can get the results you want if you are willing to put in the time and energy.

THE 20/20 EXERCISES

. . . .

I've deliberately designed the 20/20 programme to counter a great number of the 'harder' exercise alternative routines that exist: harder in terms of contact with the ground when running or in tough aerobic classes. While high-impact routines raise the heart rate very quickly, they also expose you to more damaging injuries than a low-impact training session. Repeated pounding takes its toll sooner or later, with severe strain on joints, bones and muscles.

Other factors, such as bad technique or a body not adequately prepared for stressful training, can cause injuries such as inflammation of tendons and muscles or, worse, hairline stress fractures in bones. Some will argue that a lighter training routine won't give you a proper workout, but, overall, you'll last longer and stay injury free on the lighter workout programme.

The models in the photographs in this book are not wearing shoes, as I believe that if you wear shoes it can encourage you to think you can jump and leap around without harming yourself and, as a result, people tend to be heavier on their feet. It's far better to learn balance and gentle movement, and how to be in control of your body than pounding through exercises in specially padded trainers!

FACIAL EXPRESSIONS

People underestimate the role facial expressions can play during a training session. Clenching the teeth and grimacing can often be the start of muscle and body tension.

In the bad old days this would have been seen as a way of summoning up more power; now it is just the start of a chain of events which normally leads to fatigue. For instance, clenching the teeth tightens the jaw, cramps the neck muscles and tightens the shoulders. Steadily the tension completes its journey through the lower back into the hamstrings and thighs. So remember to smile, even if you're practising your leg kick and thinking to yourself 'What do I look like?' – when you smile it is an emotional relaxer that breaks the seriousness of the exercise.

I train in front of a mirror so I can see if I am tensing up. Looking in the mirror helps me keep my jaw loose and relaxed and my breathing simple, and I find that I can pull those extra five repetitions from my body without any tension.

Correct body positioning is also much easier to achieve when performing more complicated movements in front of the mirror. There is no need to feel self-conscious either, as you don't have to worry about people staring at you. For peace of mind it is good to actually watch muscle groups at work: you can really feel the fitness beginning to flow through your body.

STRETCHING

Whenever you start an exercise programme you need to get loose and warmed up first, to ensure the muscles and joints are in working order. If you were to do aerobic/cardiovascular exercises first thing in the morning before doing any stretching you could pull a muscle.

The stretch exercises I've devised for the 20/20 programme are a workout in themselves. They cover the primary areas of the body: neck, shoulders, waist, thighs, backs of legs, hamstrings, calves and achilles tendons. The movements should be performed slowly and rhythmically, you should focus on a good range of movement, but do not try to push too far. You may want to impress your friends with how flexible you are but being super flexible is not a gold card to avoiding injury.

Look upon stretching as a body check and a way of improving flexibility throughout your body. When you do aerobic exercises the movements are generally performed too quickly to teach you anything about how your body moves. Stretching, on the other hand, is relaxed enough to give you a chance to really listen to your body.

It involves slowly stretching a muscle until you feel a little tension (which should not be confused with pain) for 10 seconds or more. You breathe in to start with and exhale as you're easing gently into the stretch hold. During a 'hold' position you will gradually feel a muscle relax and loosen slightly. These positions also have a calming effect on the body; making you ready and loose to begin the rest of the programme.

As you progress with the fitness programme you will be using muscles that may not have been used very much before, and doing stretching exercises will help to prevent them becoming stiff. On your days off from the programme, if you feel like resting then by all means rest, but if your muscles are a bit stiff then a gentle run through the stretching exercises will help them. If you've ever wondered what high muscular activity without stretching does to your body, take a look at some joggers, their hamstrings in particular tend to be very tight, and many have stiff lower back muscles.

AVOID PAIN

The last thing you want to happen is to get injured through exercising. Anything that gives pain is going to give you trouble: you need to think prevention rather than cure at all times. If you study the techniques, take your time and do not try to attain a level of fitness your body may not be ready for, then you will be fine.

I've met many people who wished that they had listened to their body when it was calling out for a rest. The exercise 'high' seems to cloud rational thinking and instead of resting for a few days, they push, bandage up and ignore. The danger is that the mind and body begin to crave the high sensation more and more, and this makes them carry on regardless when they are injured. These people are missing out on the true nature of physical health and fitness which is about feeling good inside and out, and achieving the balance between mind and body.

PROBLEM AREAS

The problem areas for most women are hips and thighs, upper arms, stomach and bottom, and for men flabby chests and stomachs. The area of the body that causes most argument is the stomach. I always impress upon my clients the importance of varying all the exercises in this area to obtain a trim and slender middle. In order to attain a stomach that looks right and feels tight, you have to work hard.

Abdominal exercising isn't easy and it requires a certain amount of mental toughness. Most people I've worked with tend to neglect their abdomen, complaining that exercising hurts and doesn't achieve results quickly enough. It is true it can be hard to make stomach muscles perform, but there are certain techniques you can incorporate to pull you through. I've designed a few new abdominal exercises in order to give the stomach an all-over flatness, but most importantly, there are over 10 different positions to help achieve maximum potential.

Women often find that even if they do lots of abdominal exercises they've still got a bulge, whereas men who perform lots of abdominal exercises end up with a nice flat rippled look. What you must remember is that men and women store fat in different places.

When men do abdominal exercises they breathe out on the effort, which makes their stomach muscles stick out, giving them the characteristic rippled look that many of them are trying to achieve. Women are not interested in looking like that, they want a much flatter, even look. I show them how to breathe out before they start the lift move, rising slowly as they approach the end of the breath.

If you want a nice flat stomach, you mustn't ignore your lower back muscles. The balance between the main abdominal muscles and the lower back muscles has to be maintained for good posture.

In the 20/20 programme I have included plenty of abdominal exercises with lots of variations in movement. Visual stimulation is good motivation when you're working out on your abdominal muscles, as in some positions you'll be able to see your stomach in better shape – the shape that you're working towards.

TENSION

Some people experience tension in the neck when doing stomach exercises. There may be several reasons for this. You could be trying too hard and, instead of keeping the jaw loose and relaxed, you're clenching your teeth, or you may be breathing incorrectly. The breathing should always be rhythmic and controlled and, if you do find the exercises tough, allow a short time to recover and then start again. If the neck muscles still continue to stiffen up, then place a cushion for support between the neck and shoulders.

Once your stomach begins to improve you will feel the difference and the tension in your neck will decrease as you begin to learn how to lift your body using just the abdominal muscles. The strength, power and will has come from within. During any abdominal workout, listen carefully to your body and if you feel any pain whatsoever in the back area stop immediately. If you're suffering from any form of back trouble, or have suffered in the past, steer clear of any abdominal exercises you think may cause you harm. The bottom is another area of the body that causes concern amongst many women. Even those who do a lot of regular exercise often complain about lack of firmness. There are plenty of machines and various treatments available which promise a lot but fail to deliver long-term changes in this area.

With the 20/20 programme, the emphasis is on thinking of the body as a whole, so while performing a leg exercise, for instance, think how you are working your bottom as well. The most successful approach is always total thinking. Take a good look at a runner in the street or park: most have developed their lower body strength but ignored their upper body. By simply introducing a variation into the arm movement which they all use, they could develop their upper bodies while performing a cardiovascular exercise like running.

This thinking of a different part of the body whilst specifically exercising another area is all part of the learning process you should adopt when working out. Spot reducing on the body is not conducive to the long-term results that everyone wants from their training. Focusing all your training time and energy on just one part of your body only increases the possibility of early drop out – so think total body for total results.

To avoid concentrating too hard on one area, try lying on your back and pointing your legs and arms in a star position (see page 63). Imagine your body slowly elongating in all four directions. This is part of the stretch programme but I often use it at the end of my training sessions to relax clients. Performing this stretch makes you really aware of your body at the end of a good workout. The signals from mind to body should tell you that you're doing well and that you can feel changes all over.

This simple stretch is also useful for relaxing the body first thing in the morning or last thing at night. Remember, mind and body should always be regarded as one; if you are mentally stressed, it will always take its toll on the body.

REACHING A PLATEAU

With any exercise plan, it is inevitable that sooner or later you will reach a plateau which will prevent you from going forward in your programme. You reach a point where no matter how hard you try, how much you push yourself, it just doesn't work. When this happens you can do one of two things – quit or coast.

Coasting is simple – it's basically going through the various movements of the exercises at a pace that suits you. If you perform the exercises at a slower speed than usual you can increase your knowledge about your body and explore important things like understanding your flexibility.

Look on it as a rehearsal for the day when you start training hard again. This shouldn't be confused with when your body feels tired. Then you have to rest and let your body recover. Coasting is rehearsing the programme to get the confidence to be able to understand what you're doing and how it's going to work for you. It can be relaxing and fun. You're free to practise movements without the adrenalin that a competitive atmosphere provides.

Coasting can help you enter a new phase of training in your programme, to get you through the plateau without losing anything you've gained in terms of looking and feeling healthier.

KEEP NOTES

I'm a real student of human movement. I always travel with a small note pad and pen, keeping track of ideas for new exercises. I look at the way people move in the street and wonder which exercises I could use to improve their gait, have I got an exercise which could do that? I never throw any of the notes away. I store them in a computer and once a month analyse every scribble and thought I've had relating to food, flexibility, strength, body definition, etc.

I try to impress upon clients to do the same. Keep track of things that come into your head, you never know what your ideas may lead to.

T H E
E X E R C I S E S

STRETCHING 44

LEGS 64

HIPS 82

UPPER BODY 90

BOTTOM 100

ABDOMINALS 110

CARDIOVASCULAR 120

The squat is an important position that is used throughout the 20/20 programme. When coming out of this stance, always remember to straighten out the legs fully.

S T R E T C H I N G

Stretching is a crucial part of my cross body training programme; it warms up the body prior to a workout and so lessens the risk of injury. It improves flexibility and so enables you to perform the other exercises more effectively. Equally, after a tough five-minute session of cardiovascular exercises, you need a period of stretching to cool down the body.

NECK MOVES

1. Looking straight ahead, relax your shoulders and position the legs shoulder-width apart with the knees bent and back straight.

2. Drop the head down, chin into chest.

3–4. Move the neck slowly and gently to the right and then to the left.

Reps: 5 each side (beginners), 10 each side (intermediate and advanced).

SHOULDER CIRCLES

1. Stand with the knees slightly bent, bottom tucked in, and gently circle the shoulders forward moving the points of the shoulders as high as you can before coming back down.

2. Repeat the exercise rolling the shoulders back.

Reps: 10 forward and 10 back (beginners), 20 forward and 20 back (intermediate and advanced).

HALF TWISTS

1. Standing as shown, bend the arms and bring them up to shoulder level.

2–3. Keeping the lower part of the body still, twist the upper body to the left, return to the start position, and twist to the right.

Reps: 10 each side (beginners), 20 each side (intermediate and advanced).

SIDE BEND

1. Take up the half-squat position as shown, remembering to keep the legs a good distance apart and the shoulders nice and relaxed.

2. Move the right leg out to the side and slowly bend sideways, keeping the back straight. Bring both arms up and reach away from the body. Hold this stretch for 10 seconds.

3. Gently lower your body down by placing the right hand on the floor for support and keeping the other arm in the raised position. Hold for 10 seconds.

4–5. Repeat the exercise on the left-
hand side, holding each position for 10
seconds.

CENTRE REACH

1. Take up the same start position as for the Side Bend (see page 48). Take your arms straight out in front and, keeping a straight back, lean forwards. Hold for 10 seconds.

2. Lower the body even further (still keeping the back straight) and reach down to the toes. Hold for 10 seconds.

When you begin stretching, remember the following points:

* Never bounce into a position.

* Ease yourself slowly into your maximum stretch position, relax then hold.

* Breathe in to start with and exhale as you go into the stretch.

* Never hold your breath when stretching.

* Always listen to your body and never push it beyond its capabilities.

3

4

3. Move the feet further apart and place the hands on the floor, palms downwards. Hold for 10 seconds.

4. Finally, clasping the elbows together, let the arms hang down in front of the body for 10 seconds. Slowly come up.

CALF STRETCH

1. Stand straight, legs together, bottom tucked in.

2. Bend the arms and raise them to shoulder level. Take one step forward keeping the heel of the back leg on the ground at all times. Remember, keep the back straight. Hold for 10 seconds. You should feel a pull in the calf of the back leg. Repeat the exercise using the other leg.

LUNGE HOLD

1. Take up the same start position as for the Calf Stretch (see opposite). Keeping the back straight and using your arms for balance, take a big step forward with the right leg. Hold for 10 seconds. Repeat using the other leg.

LUNGE SPLIT

1. Starting from the lunge position, gradually straighten the front leg and lower your chest in towards the leg. Don't worry if you can't straighten the front leg. Place the arms either side of the leg with palms on the floor. Keep the back leg straight and hold for 10 seconds.

2. Take the front leg even further forward until the knee of the back leg touches the floor. Then gradually inch the hands towards the heel of the front leg and hold for 10 seconds. Repeat on the other side.

TOE REACH

1. Sitting with legs apart, reach both arms up high.

2. Slowly come forward, keeping the back straight, and reach out towards the toes (don't worry if you can't touch them). Hold for 10 seconds.

3. Lean further forwards, if you can, and bring the arms down in front of the legs and place the hands near the ankles. Hold for 10 seconds. Do not curl your back to achieve this position, it should be straight at all times.

4. Bring the arms towards the centre and, placing your palms flat on the floor, walk your hands as far away from your body as you can. Keep the back straight. Hold for 10 seconds.

5. Move over to the right and grasp the ankle with both hands and bring your chest down towards the knee. Hold for 10 seconds and then repeat the exercise on the other side.

HAMSTRING REACH

1–2. With one leg extended and the other bent, lean forwards over the outstretched leg and, if you can do so without straining, clasp your toes. Hold the position for 10 seconds, then repeat over the other leg.

HAMSTRING STRETCH

1. Sitting on the floor, bring both legs straight out in front and reach down towards the toes. Keep the back straight. Hold for 10 seconds.

BACK ROLL

1. Sit up as shown, keeping the back nice and straight.

2. Gently roll back to the count of 10 by clasping the knees into the chest until the back is flat on the floor.

3. Unclasp the legs and place the feet on the floor, keeping the legs bent, ready for the next exercise.

LOWER BACK STRETCH

1. Lying flat on the floor, bring one leg up into the chest.

2. Pull the knee across the body using the left-hand arm. Take the other arm out straight to the side and look along the extended arm. Hold for 10 seconds. Repeat other side.

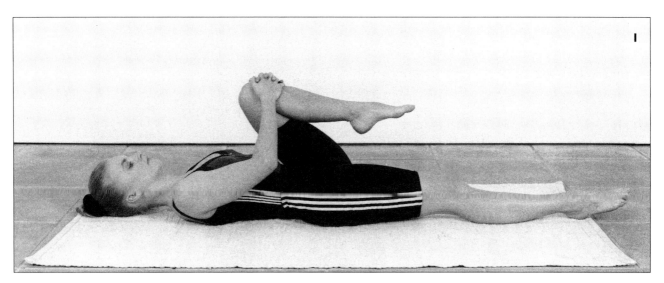

BACK AND BODY STRETCH

1. Lying flat on your back, stretch out your arms and legs as far as you can. Point the toes and extend the fingers. Hold for 20 seconds.

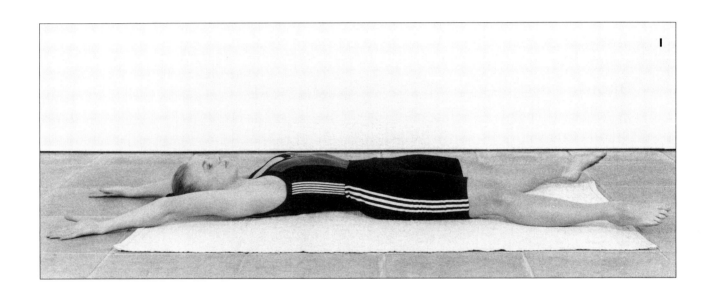

HAMSTRING STRETCH

1. Lie flat on back with knees bent.

2. Raise one leg in towards the body. Clasp the raised leg around the ankle or calf, whichever is most comfortable, and gently ease the leg further in towards the chest. Don't worry if you have to bend the leg slightly to achieve this hold. Hold for 10 seconds. Repeat using the other leg.

LEG SPLIT

1. Lying on your back, spread your legs out as wide as possible. Use the hands to gently press the legs down further. Hold for 20 seconds.

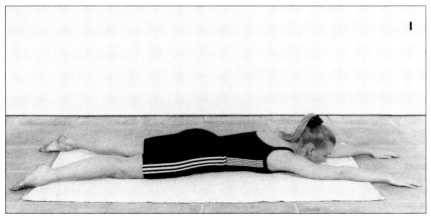

ALTERNATE LEG AND ARM RAISE

1. Lying flat on the stomach, stretch out the arms and legs with toes pointed and fingers extended.

2. Slowly raise the right arm and left leg. Lower and then raise the left arm and right leg.

Reps: 5 times each leg and arm (beginners), 10 times each leg and arm (intermediate and advanced).

UPPER BODY RAISE

1. Lying flat on the floor, take the arms out at right angles to the rest of the body.

2. Slowly raise the upper body as far as you can and then gently lower it.

Reps: 10 raises (beginners), 20 raises (intermediate and advanced).

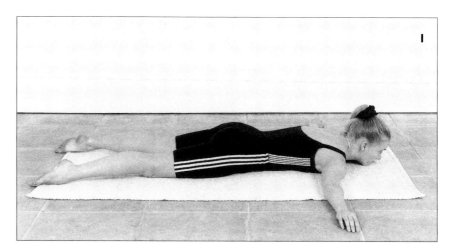

LOWER BODY RAISE

1. Starting as before, raise the lower body, keeping the upper body flat on the floor.

Reps: 10 raises (beginners), 20 raises (intermediate and advanced).

UPPER AND LOWER BODY RAISE

1. Now combine the two previous exercises by raising the upper and lower body simultaneously.

Reps: 10 raises (beginners), 20 raises (intermediate and advanced).

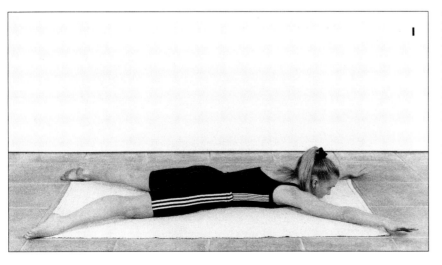

STAR STRETCH

1. This is a good exercise to do at the end of a workout session as well as at the beginning. Lying flat on the floor stretch out your arms and legs as far as you possibly can, remembering to stretch out even your fingers and toes. Hold for 20 seconds and then relax.

L E G S

• •

In order to perform these exercises effectively it is essential your balance and posture are right. The squat position is one of the key positions in this group of exercises and you must learn to position yourself correctly; keep the back straight, bottom tucked in and never squat below the knees.

Remember, a stable start position will increase your level of improvement, and, when you're required to support yourself on the floor with your hands and one leg, always make sure you keep control of the leg that's working. It's easy just to start swinging it around instead of moving it smoothly with control.

ARM SWING SQUAT

1. Stand with the feet a good shoulder-width apart and arms raised as shown.

2. Bend the knees and move down into a squat position, taking the arms straight out to the side as you go down. Remember to keep the back straight and the bottom tucked in. Return to the start position and continue.

Reps: 10 (beginners), 20 (intermediate), 30 (advanced).

SINGLE PUNCH SQUAT

1. Standing as before with the legs wide apart, punch one arm out in front with fist clenched whilst taking the other one back. Make sure you keep the arms raised at shoulder level.

2. Move down into the squat position and, as you do so, punch forward with the arm that was in the contracted position and bring the extended arm back. Return to the start position and repeat the sequence.

Reps: 10 each arm (beginners), 20 each arm (intermediate), 30 each arm (advanced).

1

DOUBLE PUNCH SQUAT

1. Stand as before, arms straight out in front with fists clenched.

2. Move down into the squat position whilst bringing both arms back. Return to the start position and continue.

Reps: 10 (beginners), 20 (intermediate), 30 (advanced).

2

SQUAT HOLDS

1. Stand with feet wide apart, arms raised straight above the head.

2. Move down into the squat position as shown and swing the arms straight out to the side so they are parallel with the shoulders. Stay in this position and raise the arms overhead with fists clenched.

Reps: 10 (beginners), 20 (intermediate), 30 (advanced).

3. Remaining in the squat position, raise one arm straight above the head and keep the other one bent at shoulder level, as shown. Then extend the bent arm up into the raised position and bring the raised arm down into the bent position and repeat.

Reps: 10 each arm (beginners), 20 each arm (intermediate), 30 each arm (advanced).

4. Again, stay in the squat position but raise both arms straight above the head. Bring both arms down into the contracted position, then extend up again.

Reps: 10 (beginners), 20 (intermediate), 30 (advanced).

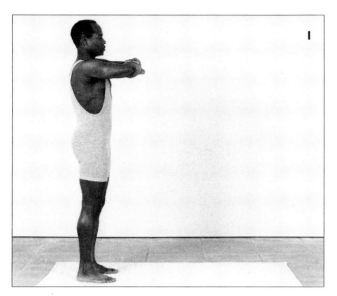

LUNGE TWIST

1. Position yourself as shown, making sure you have a good balanced position.

2. Take one large step forward so thigh is parallel to floor.

The left leg should be extended out behind with the heel facing upwards. Twist the upper body round.

Reps: 5 times each leg (beginners), 10 times each leg (intermediate), 20 times each leg (advanced).

TOE RAISE

1. Start in the squat position, arms crossed at shoulder height.

2. Raise yourself up onto the toes, as high as you can. Perform this exercise slowly so you keep your balance.

Reps: 10 (beginners), 20 (intermediate), 30 (advanced).

ARM RAISE SQUAT

1. Start in the squat position as shown with the arms raised and fists clenched.

2. Ensuring your back is straight, bring the arms down straight in front of the body. Remaining in the squat position, raise the arms straight up above the head and then lower them again.

Reps: 10 (beginners), 20 (intermediate), 30 (advanced).

SIDE LUNGE

1. Stand with the legs wide apart, feet pointing out to the side and arms raised at shoulder level.

2. Using the arms for balance, move slowly down into a squat position but take the weight of the body out to one side. Keep the heels firmly on the floor at all times.

3. Maintaining the squat position, move the upper body across to the other side. Keep the back straight throughout the sequence.

Reps: 5 each side (beginners), 10 each side (intermediate), 20 each side (advanced).

LEG KICK

1. Note how straight the start position is. Try and maintain this stance throughout and do not sacrifice it by trying to attempt a higher leg kick.

2. Bring one knee up towards the arms.

3. Kick leg out from the knee. You may well be able to straighten your leg out, unlike mine, still it just goes to show that we're all human.

Reps: 10 each leg (beginners), 20 each leg (intermediate), 30 each leg (advanced).

1

2

BODY LEG RAISE

1. Resting on your hands and feet, as shown, make sure you secure a comfortable position before raising the leg. Remember to keep the knee of the supporting leg slightly bent.

2. Raise the right leg 10 times, keeping the toes pointed. Rest and repeat using the other leg. Some of you may find this tough on the upper body as you are supporting your body weight on your arms, so just do as many repetitions as you can manage, but aim for the following:

Reps: 10 each leg (beginners), 20 each leg (intermediate), 30 each leg (advanced).

KNEELING LEG SWING

1. Supporting your body on the right knee and arm as shown, raise the left leg out to the side using the free arm for balance. Take your time getting into this start position to ensure you create a good firm support from which to begin the exercise.

2. Keeping the leg straight, toes pointed, bring it round in front of you, as far as you can.

3–4. Return to the start position and then take the leg out to the back, as far as you can.

Reps: whole sequence 10 times each side (beginners), whole sequence 20 times each side (intermediate), whole sequence 30 times each side (advanced).

TRI-LEG KICK

1. Position yourself as shown, supporting your weight on your arms and one leg. Make sure you are in a good stable position.

2. Bring the extended leg out at right angles to the body as far as you can. Keep the toes pointed.

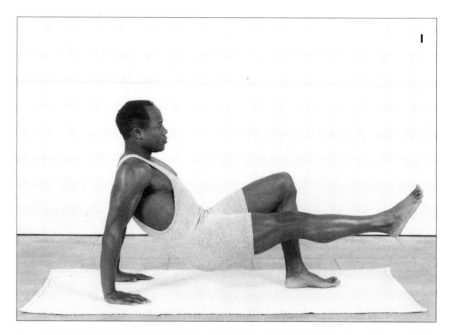

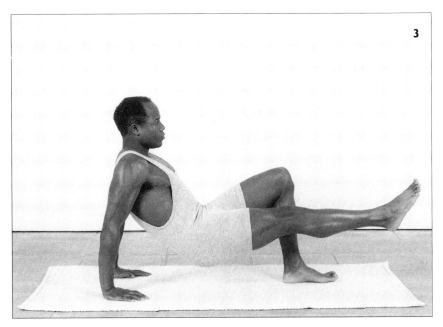

3

3–4. Take the leg back to the horizontal start position and then kick it up in the air as high as you can.

Reps: 10 each leg (beginners), 20 each leg (intermediate), 30 each leg (advanced).

4

LEG SWING

1. Kneel on the floor with one leg extended straight out behind. Keep the toes pointed.

2. Bring the leg in at right angles to the body and then return to the start position.

Reps: 10 each leg (beginners), 20 each leg (intermediate), 30 each leg (advanced).

SIDE SWING

1. Kneel on the floor with the leg raised at right angles to the body as for position 2 above. Point the toes. Swing the raised leg up and down. Repeat using the other leg.

Reps: 10 each leg (beginners), 20 each leg (intermediate), 30 each leg (advanced).

SEATED ARM AND LEG PUNCH

1–2. Coordination is the key to this exercise, so think opposite arm to opposite leg. Keeping the back straight at all times, punch forward whilst bringing the leg in towards the chest. Always bring the opposite leg in to the arm that is punching forward. Then repeat reversing the arms and legs.

Reps: 10 each leg (beginners), 20 each leg (intermediate), 30 each leg (advanced).

1

2

SLOW STEP IN

1. Support your body on your hands and feet as shown, making sure the body is aligned correctly by keeping the bottom up and the back straight.

2. Slowly bring one knee into the chest and then back again. Do not touch the floor with the foot as you bring the leg in. Take the leg back out and repeat using the other leg.

Reps: 10 each leg (beginners), 20 each leg (intermediate), 30 each leg (advanced).

LEG POINT

1. Stand as shown, with one foot facing forwards and the other out to the side.

2. Slowly move down over the right leg into a semi-squat position, taking the right arm out to the side as you do so.

3. Hold this position and look along the extended arm. Then return to a standing position.

Reps: 10 each side (beginners), 20 each side (intermediate), 30 each side (advanced).

HIPS

• •

This is a problem area for many women and it's only through hard work that changes will occur. Some of these exercises require only a small range of movement but are nevertheless extremely effective, so don't increase the range of movement.

It is important to get the start position right. If you don't, then you will decrease the effectiveness of the exercises, so follow the directions carefully.

HIP CIRCLE

1. Lean against the wall as shown.

2–3. Circle the raised leg forward, keeping the foot flexed.
Aim to make this circling motion as large as possible.
Reps: 15 each leg (beginners), 20 each leg (intermediate),
30 each leg (advanced).

HIP KICK

1. Position as shown, keeping the back and raised leg in a straight line. Flex the foot.

2–3. Bring the raised leg forwards until it is at right angles to the body and then take it back to the start position.

Reps: 20 each leg (beginners), 30 each leg (intermediate), 40 each leg (advanced).

HIP LIFT

1. Lean against the wall and raise one leg out to the side.

2. Lower the raised leg down towards the floor and then bring it up again.

Reps: 20 each leg (beginners), 30 each leg (intermediate), 40 each leg (advanced).

HIP SWING

1. Position as shown. Start with the leg raised at right angles to the body, foot flexed.

2. Swing the raised leg in towards the shoulder as far as you can.

Reps: 10 each leg (beginners), 20 each leg (intermediate), 30 each leg (advanced).

KNEELING HIP CIRCLE

1. Kneel down as shown and raise one leg out to the side.

2. Circle the raised leg forwards, keeping the foot flexed.

Reps: 20 each leg (beginners), 30 each leg (intermediate), 40 each leg (advanced).

KNEELING HIP SWING

1. Kneel down, leaning against a wall, and raise one leg straight out behind. Keep the foot flexed.

2. Swing the raised leg in towards the shoulder, keeping it at least a foot above the ground.

Reps: 10 each leg (beginners), 20 each leg (intermediate), 30 each leg (advanced).

KNEELING HIP RAISE

1–2. Kneel down as shown and raise one leg out to the side as far as you can. Then lower it. Try not to lean over to one side as you do this exercise, remembering to let the hips do the work. If you do find yourself starting to lean then it's probably because you're trying to raise the leg too high.

Reps: 20 each leg (beginners), 30 each leg (intermediate), 40 each leg (advanced).

KNEELING HIP KICK

1. Kneel down, keeping the back straight with the hands flat against the wall at about shoulder height.

2–3. Swing one leg out behind, keeping the leg bent and the foot flexed at all times. Return to the start position and continue. Unfortunately, you won't have me there to help you.

Reps: 20 each leg (beginners), 30 each leg (intermediate), 40 each leg (advanced).

U P P E R   B O D Y

• •

Women will find the upper body exercises particularly tough but they are worth persevering with to get rid of those flabby upper arms. These exercises are all about supporting your own body weight. Gradually you will gain strength and your definition will improve. Technique is all important so study the start positions carefully and make sure your body positioning is correct. The main aim is to perform these exercises safely and efficiently: if you are really having to strain to do these exercises then check your technique.

* When performing these exercises, breathe out as you exert yourself and in as you relax.

SINGLE AND DOUBLE PUNCHES OVERHEAD

1. Kneel down, keeping the body straight. Raise the arms to shoulder level and bend. Clench the fists.

2. You are now going to do a series of single arm punches by extending one arm straight up above your head and keeping the other arm bent. Repeat this sequence by bringing the extended arm down and raising the bent arm.
Reps: 20 each arm (beginners), 30 each arm (intermediate), 40 each arm (advanced).

3. Now do a series of double punches overhead by extending both arms up above the head and bringing them down into the contracted position.
Reps: 20 (beginners), 30 (intermediate), 40 (advanced).

90

SINGLE AND DOUBLE FORWARD PUNCHES

1–2. Note the start position for the forward punches. Make sure when you take your arms back that the top part of the arms are parallel with the shoulders. Don't let them drop down.

3. You should now be familiar with these exercises, so, remembering to keep the back nice and straight, punch forward with alternate arms.

4. Follow this up with a series of double forward punches. Yes, I know it's hard but keep going. Just think, no more flabby arms.

Reps: 20 each arm (beginners), 30 each arm (intermediate), 40 each arm (advanced).

HAND WALK

1. Supporting your body on your feet and hands, keep your back straight and bottom up. This is very important as you can damage your back if you let it sag.

2–4. Keeping the hands wide apart, take 2 steps to the right, then return to the centre and take 2 steps to the left.

Reps: whole sequence 5 times (beginners), whole sequence 10 times (intermediate), whole sequence 15 times (advanced).

WALL PRESS-UPS

1. Kneeling down, place your hands against the wall making sure they are more than shoulder-width apart. Keep the arms slightly bent.

2. Gently lean in towards the wall, taking the weight of your body on your arms as you do so.

Reps: 10 (beginners), 20 (intermediate), 30 (advanced).

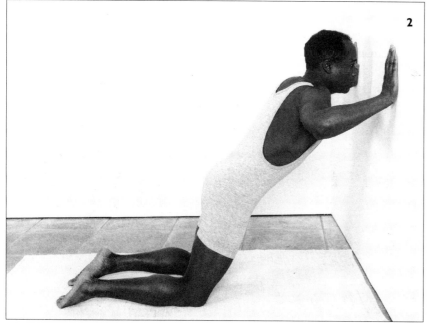

PUSH-UP VARIATIONS

1. Men, who have more upper body strength, should go for my positioning with the arms and feet wide apart whilst women should keep a narrower stance as shown.

2. Men, lower the body as far as you can go! It may look as if I am touching the floor, but I'm not.

3

3–4. Here you can see the same positions from the side. Note how low I manage to go.

Reps (men only): 20 (beginners), 30 (intermediate), 40 (advanced).

4

5. Women should only attempt a small range of movement. Make sure you imitate Kari's start position accurately, keeping the arms bent and the bottom raised above the head and shoulders. The hands should be positioned so they are in front of the shoulders.

6. This side view shows how you should keep the bottom above shoulder level. Slowly bend the arms and move forward.

Reps (women only): 10 (beginners), 20 (intermediate), 30 (advanced).

UPPER BODY LIFT

1. Lying on the floor, keep your elbows tucked in and hands flat on the floor. Bend the knees.

2. Raise the body up on your elbows until your bottom is at least 6 inches off the ground.

Reps: 20 (beginners), 30 (intermediate), 40 (advanced).

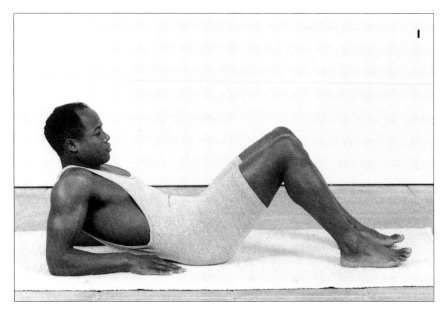

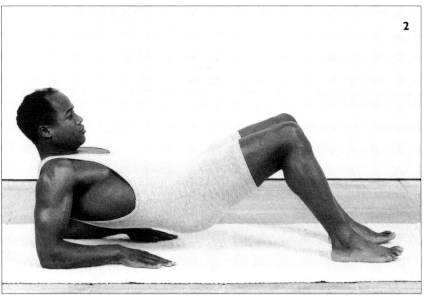

TRICEP PUSHES

1. Sit as shown, keeping the arms bent.

2–3. Then raise the body up by slowly straightening the arms. Lower the body and continue.

Reps: 10 (beginners), 20 (intermediate), 30 (advanced).

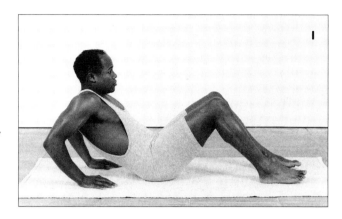

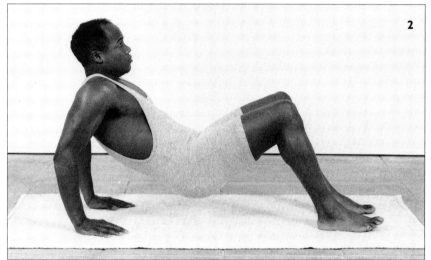

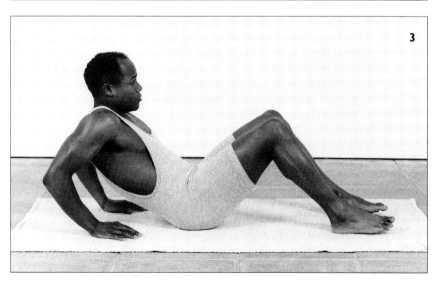

BOTTOM

The most important thing to remember throughout these exercises is to keep the bottom squeezed tight whilst performing the movements. Don't squeeze it so tightly that your ability to move is restricted but keep a constant tension.

Remember to breath in as you go into the movement and out as your exert yourself.

LEG AND BOTTOM TIGHTENER

1. Kneeling on all fours, take one leg out behind, making sure it forms a continuous line with the back. This is when a mirror is useful to check your positioning.

2. Bring the extended leg round until it is at right angles with the rest of the body. Make sure you keep the foot flexed as you do this and that you squeeze the buttocks together.

3–4. Take the leg back round and kick up as far as you can, keeping control of the movement and your balance. Point the toe as you perform this last phase of the exercise.

Reps: whole sequence 20 times each leg (beginners), whole sequence 30 times each leg (intermediate), whole sequence 40 times each leg (advanced).

SIDE SWING

1. Support your body on your hands and feet as shown, making sure your start position is secure.

2. Slowly, with a controlled movement, swing one leg out to the side. Keep it level with the hips and do not touch the floor. Then bring it back to the centre and take the other leg out to the side, squeezing the buttocks together the whole time. Remember this should be a smooth, controlled action.

Reps: 10 each leg (beginners), 20 each leg (intermediate), 30 each leg (advanced).

LEG AND
BOTTOM LIFT

1. Lie as shown.

2. Keeping the upper body on the floor, squeeze the buttocks together and try and raise the thighs off the ground.

Reps: 20 (beginners), 30 (intermediate), 40 (advanced).

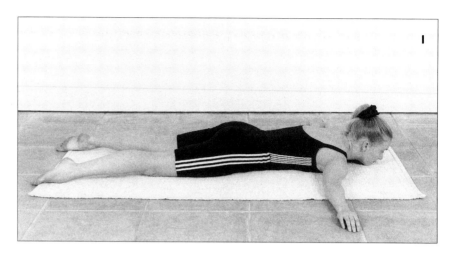

PELVIC LIFT

1. To do this exercise effectively there is very little movement. Lie up against the wall as shown.

2. Squeeze the buttocks and pelvic floor muscles together and in so doing you should raise the bottom a few inches off the ground. Relax the muscles and continue.

Reps: 30 (beginners), 40 (intermediate), 50 (advanced).

BOTTOM AND THIGH SQUEEZE

1. Keep the head, back and arms flat against the wall, legs slightly bent.

2. Squeeze the bottom and raise one leg, with the knee bent, in towards the chest.

Reps: 10 each leg (beginners), 20 each leg (intermediate), 30 each leg (advanced).

SIDE LIFT

(Opposite page, below)

1. Stand up against a wall as shown.

2. Take the leg out to the side as far as you can, tightening the bottom as you do so.

Reps: 20 each leg (beginners), 30 each leg (intermediate), 40 each leg (advanced).

SWING BACK

1–2. Stand as before but this time take the leg out behind. You won't be able to achieve as great a range of movement as before but this exercise is extremely effective in tightening up the bottom. You should raise the leg no higher than 2 feet off the ground.

Reps: 20 each leg (beginners), 30 each leg (intermediate), 40 each leg (advanced).

SQUAT

1. In order to do this exercise effectively it is extremely important to maintain the correct posture. Place your feet about shoulder-width apart, keep the back straight and tilt the pelvis forward. Fold the arms and raise up to shoulder level.

2. Squeeze the buttocks together as you go down into the semi-squat position. Do not squat below the knee.

Reps: 20 (beginners), 30 (intermediate), 40 (advanced).

BOTTOM TIGHTENER

1. Position the body as in the previous exercise. Squeeze together the buttocks and bring one knee up towards the arms.

2. Extend the leg straight out in front of you. Don't worry if it isn't completely straight.

Reps: 20 each leg (beginners), 30 each leg (intermediate), 40 each leg (advanced).

SQUAT TWIST

1. Squat down with the legs wide apart, back straight and bottom tucked in.

2–3. Keep the bottom muscles tight and twist the upper body to the right and then to the left. Make sure your lower body keeps absolutely still as you perform these twists.

Reps: 10 each side (beginners), 20 each side (intermediate), 30 each side (advanced).

SQUAT PUNCHES

1. All these exercises are performed with the body in the squat position. Remember to keep your legs wide apart and your bottom tucked in.

2. Squeezing the buttocks together, start with a series of single overhead punches.

3. Follow this with a series of double overhead punches.

Reps: 20 (beginners), 30 (intermediate), 40 (advanced).

4. Stand as shown.

5. Punch one arm forward and begin a group of single forward punches.

Reps: 20 each arm (beginners), 30 each arm (intermediate), 40 each arm (advanced).

6. Maintaining the squat position and keeping the buttocks squeezed together, finish the sequence with a group of double forward punches.

Reps: 20 (beginners), 30 (intermediate), 40 (advanced).

ABDOMINALS

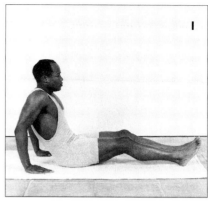

You may find that if your stomach muscles are weak you'll feel tension in the neck when raising your shoulders off the floor. To counteract this, keep the jaw slightly open and maintain a relaxed expression. Keep the head raised with the chin in towards the chest. No clenching of the teeth which causes tension in the neck. Use a cushion to support the neck if it helps.

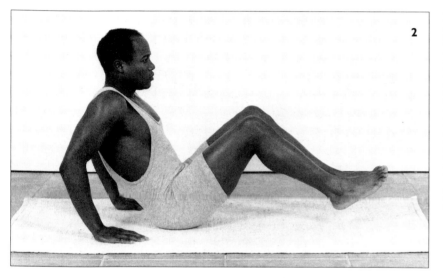

ABDOMINAL KICK

1. Sit up as shown, supporting yourself with slightly bent arms.

2–3. Lift both feet off the ground a couple of inches and bring the knees in towards the chest.

Reps: 10 (beginners), 20 (intermediate), 30 (advanced).

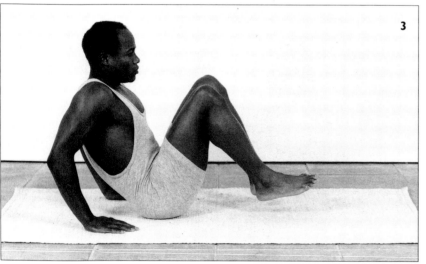

ABDOMINAL THROW

1. Lie flat out on the floor making sure the lower back is flat on the floor. Stretch out the arms.

2. Throw the arms forward to raise the body up whilst bringing one knee in towards the chest.

3. Finish the movement by clasping the raised leg into the chest.

Reps: 10 each leg (beginners), 20 each leg (intermediate), 30 each leg (advanced).

When training women I always tell them to breathe in during the strenuous phase of abdominal exercises, for example, when performing the Oblique Throw (page 114) you should inhale as you raise the body up and out as you lower the body. You may find this odd to begin with as it is the opposite way to the normal method of breathing. However, it does result in a more feminine look to the stomach whereas the more conventional breathing technique can result in protruding abdominal muscles (the rippled effect that so many men desire).

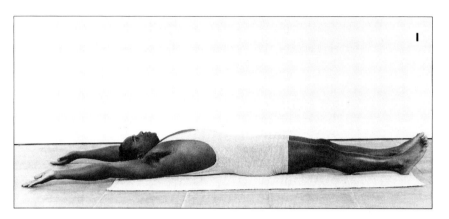

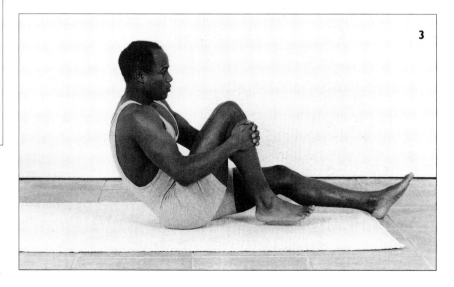

DOUBLE ABDOMINAL THROW

1–2. Start from the lying position again and throw both arms forward to raise the upper body whilst bringing your knees in towards the chest.

3. Clasp the knees into the chest. Keep the feet a couple of inches off the ground at all times.

Reps: 10 (beginners), 20 (intermediate), 30 (advanced).

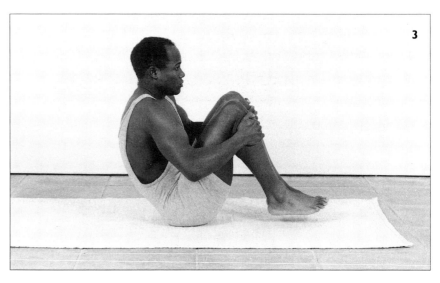

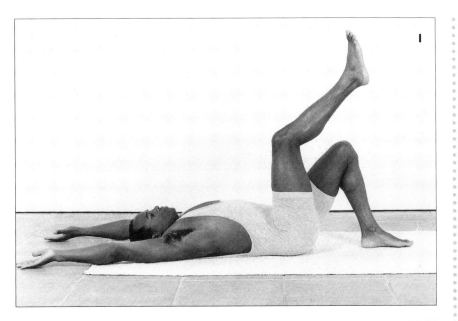

ABDOMINAL KNEE DIP

1. Lie flat on your back, one leg bent and the other leg raised, knee slightly bent. Remember to keep the lower back pressed into the floor.

2. Keeping the legs in the same position, throw the arms up either side of the raised leg and bring the shoulders off the ground. Dip the raised knee in slightly as you come up.

Reps: 10 each leg (beginners), 20 each leg (intermediate), 30 each leg (advanced).

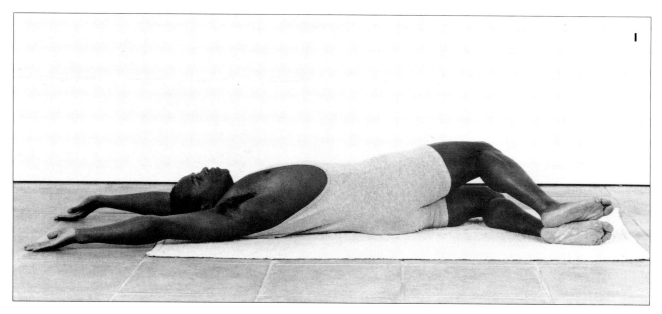

OBLIQUE THROW

1. Lie on the floor as shown. You should feel this exercise down your side. If you don't feel it, your start position is incorrect.

2. Raise the arms up over the head and take them straight out towards the heels of your feet. You are aiming to raise the shoulders off the floor.

Reps: 20 each side (beginners), 30 each side (intermediate), 40 each side (advanced).

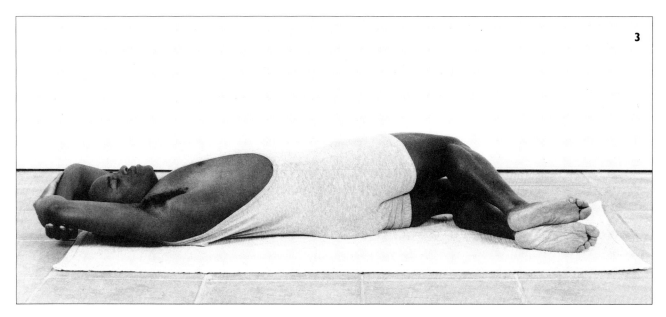

3–4. Repeat the previous exercise but with the arms clasped. Remember to keep the chin into the chest which should prevent your neck from hurting, but if it does begin to ache, relax and start again.

Reps: 20 each side (beginners), 30 each side (intermediate), 40 each side (advanced).

STEP ACROSS

1. Position as shown, keeping the bottom nice and high.

2–3. Bring one leg in and across the body without touching the ground. Take the leg back out and repeat using the other leg. You should feel this exercise in the lower abdomen which very rarely gets exercised. It's tough so be careful how you go.

Reps: 5 each leg (beginners), 10 each leg (intermediate), 15 each leg (advanced).

ABDOMINALS

1

2

ABDOMINAL WALK

1. Lie flat on your back and raise your arms and legs up in the air, keeping the legs slightly bent at all times and the lower back flat against the floor.

2. Raise the head up, keeping the chin into the chest. If your neck hurts then support it with a cushion. Swing alternate legs and arms in a walking motion.

Reps: 10 each side (beginners), 20 each side (intermediate), 30 each side (advanced).

1

2

ABDOMINAL PUNCHES

1–2. Lying down, punch across the body whilst bringing the right knee up and in. Raise the shoulders off the ground. Then repeat the other side bringing the left knee in.

Reps: 10 each side (beginners), 20 each side (intermediate), 30 each side (advanced).

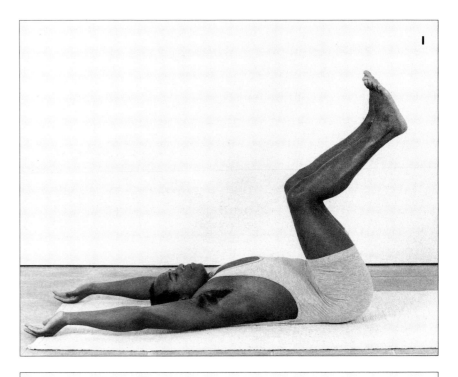

DOUBLE KNEE DIP

1. Lie as shown. Make sure you keep your spine pushed into the floor.

2. Bring your arms up towards your bended knees and raise the head and shoulders off the ground.

Reps: 10 (beginners), 20 (intermediate), 30 (advanced).

CARDIOVASCULAR

. . . .

Although there are only five exercises in this section, grouped together they provide a great workout for improving your aerobic/cardiovascular endurance. They should, ideally, be performed quickly but you would be well advised to rehearse them slowly beforehand. Technique is all important if you are to perform these movements quickly but with control. Never exert yourself to the point where you lose your composure and work at your own pace.

SIDE STEP

1–2. Support your body using your hands and feet as shown. Make sure you keep the back straight.

3. Take one leg out to the side and then bring it in to the centre again. Repeat using the other leg.

Reps: 30 each leg (beginners), 40 each leg (intermediate), 50 each leg (advanced).

STEPPING IN AND OUT

1. Position as shown, keeping the back and arms straight.

2. Step in with one leg, bringing the knee as near to the arms as possible.

3. Return to the start position and repeat using the other leg. The foot should touch the ground lightly and the whole exercise should be performed with control.

Reps: 30 each leg (beginners), 40 each leg (intermediate), 50 each leg (advanced).

HIGH STEP

1. This is *not* running on the spot. Lift the right leg as high as you can across your body and come up onto your toes as you do so. Swing the arms out to the other side to balance yourself.

2. Repeat the exercise using the other leg. Remember to try and relax your face – it looks as if I was giving Kari a bit of a tough time here!

Reps: 20 each leg (beginners), 30 each leg (intermediate), 40 each leg (advanced).

KNEE PUSH

1. Support your body as shown.

2. Bring one knee forward in towards the chest. Do not touch the ground.

3. Take the leg back and bring the other leg in. This exercise should be performed quickly.

Reps: 20 each leg (beginners), 30 each leg (intermediate), 40 each leg (advanced).

CARDIO REACH

1. Squat down with arms straight down in front of body.

2–3. Come up, with a straight back, right up on to your toes with arms outstretched.

Reps: 10 (beginners), 20 (intermediate), 30 (advanced).

SECTION 6

THE 20/20 PROGRAMMES

. . . .

I have devised three programmes on the following pages; one for beginners, the basic 20/20 programme; one for those who are already fairly fit – the 20/20 Intermediate Programme; and one for those who fancy a real challenge and are seriously fit – the 20/20 Advanced Programme. Even if you are in good condition and scored over 100 on the fitness questionnaire (page 25), you would still be advised to start with the intermediate programme as the advanced one is an extremely tough 40-minute workout.

It is important when following the programmes to go at your own pace and listen to your body – if you are in pain STOP. The workouts are divided into five-minute sections (ten if you're doing the advanced programme) each concentrating on a particular area of the body, for example, the legs. Don't worry if you can't complete all the leg/hip/bottom exercises in the time available. Keep a note of where you reached and continue from that point next time that particular group of exercises come up. In this way you shouldn't get bored as there are always plenty of new exercises.

The charts on pages 126–130 give a summary of all the exercises, plus the suggested number of repetitions for each of the programmes. You can quickly refer to it and see at a glance how many exercises are in each group, and how many you managed to get through. Good luck.

STRETCHING EXERCISES

NUMBER OF REPETITIONS/LENGTH OF HOLD

	Beginners' Programme	Intermediate Programme	Advanced Programme	
1 NECK MOVES	5	10	10	EACH SIDE
2 SHOULDER CIRCLES	10	20	20	EACH SIDE
3 HALF TWISTS	10	20	20	EACH SIDE
4 SIDE BEND	HOLD EACH POSITION FOR 10 SECONDS			
5 CENTRE REACH	HOLD EACH POSITION FOR 10 SECONDS			
6 CALF STRETCH	HOLD FOR 10 SECONDS			
7 LUNGE HOLD	HOLD EACH SIDE FOR 10 SECONDS			
8 LUNGE SPLIT	HOLD EACH SIDE FOR 10 SECONDS			
9 TOE REACH	HOLD EACH POSITION FOR 10 SECONDS			
10 HAMSTRING REACH	HOLD EACH LEG FOR 10 SECONDS			
11 HAMSTRING STRETCH	HOLD FOR 10 SECONDS			
12 BACK ROLL	ROLL DOWN TO COUNT OF 10			
13 LOWER BACK STRETCH	HOLD EACH LEG FOR 10 SECONDS			
14 BACK AND BODY STRETCH	HOLD FOR 20 SECONDS			
15 HAMSTRING STRETCH	HOLD FOR 10 SECONDS			
16 LEG SPLIT	HOLD FOR 20 SECONDS			
17 ALTERNATE LEG AND ARM RAISE	5	10	10	EACH LEG AND ARM
18 UPPER BODY RAISE	10	20	20	
19 LOWER BODY RAISE	10	20	20	
20 UPPER AND LOWER BODY RAISE	10	20	20	
21 STAR STRETCH	HOLD FOR 20 SECONDS			

LEG EXERCISES

NUMBER OF REPETITIONS

	Beginners' Programme	Intermediate Programme	Advanced Programme	
1 ARM SWING SQUAT	10	20	30	
2 SINGLE PUNCH SQUAT	10	20	30	EACH ARM
3 DOUBLE PUNCH SQUAT	10	20	30	
4 SQUAT HOLDS	10	20	30	EACH ARM (where relevant)
5 LUNGE TWIST	5	10	20	EACH LEG
6 TOE RAISE	10	20	30	
7 ARM RAISE SQUAT	10	20	30	
8 SIDE LUNGE	5	10	20	EACH SIDE
9 LEG KICK	10	20	30	EACH LEG
10 BODY LEG RAISE	10	20	30	EACH LEG
11 KNEELING LEG SWING	10	20	30	EACH SIDE
12 TRI-LEG KICK	10	20	30	EACH LEG
13 LEG SWING	10	20	30	EACH LEG
14 SIDE SWING	10	20	30	EACH LEG
15 SEATED ARM AND LEG PUNCH	10	20	30	EACH LEG
16 SLOW STEP IN	10	20	30	EACH LEG
17 LEG POINT	10	20	30	EACH SIDE

HIP EXERCISES
NUMBER OF REPETITIONS

	Beginners' Programme	Intermediate Programme	Advanced Programme	
1 HIP CIRCLE	15	20	30	EACH LEG
2 HIP KICK	20	30	40	EACH LEG
3 HIP LIFT	20	30	40	EACH LEG
4 HIP SWING	10	20	30	EACH LEG
5 KNEELING HIP CIRCLE	20	30	40	EACH LEG
6 KNEELING HIP SWING	10	20	30	EACH LEG
7 KNEELING HIP RAISE	20	30	40	EACH LEG
8 KNEELING HIP KICK	20	30	40	EACH LEG

UPPER BODY EXERCISES
NUMBER OF REPETITIONS

	Beginners' Programme	Intermediate Programme	Advanced Programme	
1 SINGLE PUNCHES OVERHEAD	20	30	40	EACH ARM
2 DOUBLE PUNCHES OVERHEAD	20	30	40	
3 SINGLE PUNCHES FORWARD	20	30	40	EACH ARM
4 DOUBLE PUNCHES FORWARD	20	30	40	
5 HAND WALK	5	10	15	
6 WALL PRESS-UPS	10	20	30	
7 PUSH-UP VARIATIONS	20 (MEN) 10 (WOMEN)	30 (MEN) 20 (WOMEN)	40 (MEN) 30 (WOMEN)	
8 UPPER BODY LIFT	20	30	40	
9 TRICEP PUSHES	10	20	30	

BOTTOM EXERCISES

NUMBER OF REPETITIONS

	Beginners' Programme	Intermediate Programme	Advanced Programme	
1 LEG AND BOTTOM TIGHTENER	20	30	40	EACH LEG
2 SIDE SWING	10	20	30	EACH LEG
3 LEG AND BOTTOM LIFT	20	30	40	
4 PELVIC LIFT	30	40	50	
5 BOTTOM AND THIGH SQUEEZE	10	20	30	EACH LEG
6 SIDE LIFT	20	30	40	EACH LEG
7 SWING BACK	20	30	40	EACH LEG
8 SQUAT	20	30	40	
9 BOTTOM TIGHTENER	20	30	40	EACH LEG
10 SQUAT TWISTS	10	20	30	EACH SIDE
11 SQUAT PUNCHES	20	30	40	

ONE ON ONE

ABDOMINAL EXERCISES
NUMBER OF REPETITIONS

	Beginners' Programme		Intermediate Programme	Advanced Programme
1 ABDOMINAL KICK	10	20	30	
2 ABDOMINAL THROW	10	20	30	EACH LEG
3 DOUBLE ABDOMINAL THROW	10	20	30	
4 ABDOMINAL KNEE DIP	10	20	30	EACH LEG
5 OBLIQUE THROW	20	30	40	EACH SIDE
6 STEP ACROSS	5 10	15	EACH LEG	
7 ABDOMINAL WALK	10	20	30	EACH SIDE
8 ABDOMINAL PUNCHES	10	20	30	EACH SIDE
9 DOUBLE KNEE DIP	10	20	30	

CARDIOVASCULAR EXERCISES
NUMBER OF REPETITIONS

	Beginners' Programme	Intermediate Programme	Advanced Programme	
1 SIDE STEP	30	40	50	EACH LEG
2 STEPPING IN AND OUT	30	40	50	EACH LEG
3 HIGH STEP	20	30	40	EACH LEG
4 KNEE PUSH	20	30	40	EACH LEG
5 CARDIO REACH	10	20	30	

THE 20/20 BEGINNERS' PROGRAMME

20 MINUTES A DAY FOR 20 DAYS

This basic programme is aimed at beginners and involves only 20 minutes exercising per day with two rest days every five days: these can be taken consecutively or split according to how you feel and your time schedule.

Each day is broken up into five-minute sections with each period spent exercising a different part of the body. Everyday starts off with five minutes of stretching. Remember, don't worry if you can't get through all the exercises in one five-minute session: it doesn't matter, simply start the next session where you left off.

The first five days of exercise are deliberately 'easy' and include two five-minute periods of stretching: the aim is to break you gently into the programme so you're not in agony and give up after day three!

Note Each day is divided into five-minute exercise sections, totalling 20 minutes a day. A five-minute period of stretching always follows the cardiovascular exercises to allow the body to cool down.

DAY 3

STRETCH
LEGS
CARDIOVASCULAR
STRETCH

DAY 6

STRETCH
ABDOMINALS
BOTTOM
UPPER BODY

DAY I

STRETCH (5 MINS.)
BOTTOM (5 MINS.)
CARDIOVASCULAR (5 MINS.)
STRETCH (5 MINS.)

DAY 4

STRETCH
UPPER BODY
HIPS
STRETCH

DAY 7

STRETCH
HIPS
CARDIOVASCULAR
STRETCH

DAY 2

STRETCH
UPPER BODY
ABDOMINALS
STRETCH

DAY 5

STRETCH
ABDOMINALS
BOTTOM
STRETCH

DAY 8

STRETCH
LEGS
ABDOMINALS
BOTTOM

——— 2 REST DAYS ———

ONE ON ONE

DAY 9

STRETCH
UPPER BODY
CARDIOVASCULAR
STRETCH

DAY 10

STRETCH
HIPS
ABDOMINALS
LEGS

2 REST DAYS

DAY 11

STRETCH
UPPER BODY
CARDIOVASCULAR
STRETCH

DAY 12

STRETCH
BOTTOM
ABDOMINALS
LEGS

DAY 13

STRETCH
HIPS
CARDIOVASCULAR
STRETCH

DAY 14

STRETCH
LEGS
ABDOMINALS
BOTTOM

DAY 15

STRETCH
UPPER BODY
CARDIOVASCULAR
STRETCH

2 REST DAYS

DAY 16

STRETCH
HIPS
ABDOMINALS
BOTTOM

DAY 17

STRETCH
LEGS
CARDIOVASCULAR
STRETCH

DAY 18

STRETCH
UPPER BODY
HIPS
ABDOMINALS

DAY 19

STRETCH
BOTTOM
CARDIOVASCULAR
STRETCH

DAY 20

STRETCH
LEGS
ABDOMINALS
UPPER BODY

2 REST DAYS

THE 20/20 INTERMEDIATE PROGRAMME

20 MINUTES EVERY OTHER DAY

If you have completed the 20-day Beginners' Programme or have scored well on the fitness questionnaire (see page 25) then you are now ready for the intermediate programme. This, more strenuous programme, involves an increased number of repetitions and I therefore recommend exercising only every other day over a 40 day period.

If you still find the beginners' programme hard then don't begin this one — wait until you find it relatively easy.

Note Each day is divided into five-minute exercise sections, totalling 20 minutes a day.

DAY 1	DAY 7	DAY 13
STRETCH (5 MINS.)	STRETCH	STRETCH
LEGS (5 MINS.)	LEGS	BOTTOM
ABDOMINALS (5 MINS.)	CARDIOVASCULAR	ABDOMINALS
UPPER BODY (5 MINS.)	STRETCH	LEGS

DAY 3	DAY 9	DAY 15
STRETCH	STRETCH	STRETCH
BOTTOM	HIPS	HIPS
CARDIOVASCULAR	ABDOMINALS	CARDIOVASCULAR
STRETCH	BOTTOM	STRETCH

DAY 5	DAY 11	DAY 17
STRETCH	STRETCH	STRETCH
UPPER BODY	UPPER BODY	LEGS
HIPS	CARDIOVASCULAR	UPPER BODY
ABDOMINALS	STRETCH	BOTTOM

DAY 19

STRETCH
ABDOMINALS
CARDIOVASCULAR
STRETCH

DAY 21

STRETCH
HIPS
BOTTOM
LEGS

DAY 23

STRETCH
UPPER BODY
CARDIOVASCULAR
STRETCH

DAY 25

STRETCH
LEGS
ABDOMINALS
BOTTOM

DAY 27

STRETCH
HIPS
CARDIOVASCULAR
STRETCH

DAY 29

STRETCH
ABDOMINALS
UPPER BODY
BOTTOM

DAY 31

STRETCH
LEGS
CARDIOVASCULAR
STRETCH

DAY 33

STRETCH
HIPS
ABDOMINALS
UPPER BODY

DAY 35

STRETCH
LEGS
CARDIOVASCULAR
STRETCH

DAY 37

STRETCH
BOTTOM
UPPER BODY
HIPS

DAY 39

STRETCH
ABDOMINALS
CARDIOVASCULAR
STRETCH

THE 20/20 ADVANCED PROGRAMME

40 MINUTES A DAY FOR 20 DAYS

If you have successfully completed the previous two programmes then you are ready for the advanced programme. Remember, even if you scored extremely well on the fitness questionnaire (see page 25) you would be advised to start with the intermediate programme.

This programme begins with a five-minute stretching period at the beginning and end of every 40-minute session. The rest of the time is divided into ten-minute sections, exercising a specific part of the body.

Note for the 40-minute programme each day is divided into ten-minute exercise sections with the stretching section split into five-minute periods at the beginning and end of each session.

DAY 1

STRETCH (5 MINS.)
BOTTOM (10 MINS.)
ABDOMINALS (10 MINS.)
CARDIOVASCULAR (10 MINS.)
STRETCH (5 MINS.)

DAY 2

STRETCH
HIPS
UPPER BODY
LEGS
STRETCH

DAY 3

STRETCH
ABDOMINALS
BOTTOM
HIPS
STRETCH

DAY 4

STRETCH
LEGS
UPPER BODY
BOTTOM
STRETCH

DAY 5

STRETCH
UPPER BODY
ABDOMINALS
CARDIOVASCULAR
STRETCH

DAY 6

STRETCH
BOTTOM
LEGS
UPPER BODY
STRETCH

DAY 7

STRETCH
HIPS
ABDOMINALS
CARDIOVASCULAR
STRETCH

DAY 8

STRETCH
BOTTOM
HIPS
LEGS
STRETCH

2 REST DAYS

DAY 9

STRETCH
UPPER BODY
BOTTOM
CARDIOVASCULAR
STRETCH

DAY 10

STRETCH
BOTTOM
HIPS
UPPER BODY
STRETCH

2 REST DAYS

DAY 11

STRETCH
UPPER BODY
LEGS
CARDIOVASCULAR
STRETCH

DAY 12

STRETCH
BOTTOM
ABDOMINALS
LEGS
STRETCH

DAY 13

STRETCH
UPPER BODY
ABDOMINALS
HIPS
STRETCH

DAY 14

STRETCH
HIPS
BOTTOM
CARDIOVASCULAR
STRETCH

DAY 15

STRETCH
ABDOMINALS
LEGS
UPPER BODY
STRETCH

2 REST DAYS

DAY 16

STRETCH
LEGS
HIPS
CARDIOVASCULAR
STRETCH

DAY 17

STRETCH
ABDOMINALS
BOTTOM
UPPER BODY
STRETCH

DAY 18

STRETCH
BOTTOM
LEGS
CARDIOVASCULAR
STRETCH

DAY 19

STRETCH
HIPS
UPPER BODY
CARDIOVASCULAR
STRETCH

DAY 20

STRETCH
LEGS
ABDOMINALS
CARDIOVASCULAR
STRETCH

2 REST DAYS

SECTION 7

THE 20/20 EATING PLAN

• •

If you want to get in shape, at some point you'll need to look at what you eat. I think food is great, I love eating, and, being single, I cook for myself and really enjoy trying different recipes. But I also look on it as fuel for my body to absorb to make sure I'm at my best when I'm ready to train.

I'm constantly asked what I eat day to day. I eat three meals a day, breakfast, lunch and dinner, and I try not to snack between meals. If I'm in heavy training I eat lots of pasta, raw vegetables, fish and fruit. I don't eat red meat. I don't drink alcohol but instead I drink lots of still water, at least a litre a day. I eat for energy, my food sets me up for my work schedule and my training. In winter I work out seven days a week and I'm fresh every morning after six hours sleep. I don't take vitamins as I believe there's no need to take them if you eat sensibly with lots of variety in your diet. A balanced healthy eating plan will cover anything that vitamin pills will give you, and a lot more.

I always have long discussions with my clients about food – they've all tried to lose weight by dieting, with little or no success. I never put anyone on a diet as I don't believe they work in the long run. We are all bombarded with suggestions for new ways of losing weight in record time, but it's now widely accepted that you can only suppress your natural food instincts for so long, sooner or later you will break the discipline and start eating your favourite foods all over again.

I don't tell people what they should eat. I ask them about their eating habits and make suggestions as to how they can improve them. I don't believe in calorie counting. I don't know how many calories I eat in a day and I can't think of anything more soul-destroying than trying to count the number of calories on the plate in front of me. That's taking away all the fun and enjoyment from food. If you are eating healthily, you don't need to count calories; if you're eating junk food then the last thing you need to know is how much junk – it will just make you feel more depressed and guilty than you already are. So, no calorie counting on the 20/20 programme.

I tell people they must always have breakfast, even if it is just some fruit. Don't overeat at any meals, no matter how healthy the food is, it will only slow you down. If you must eat between meals, make it something light. If you get hungry before a workout, don't eat just before but give yourself at least three hours, and, again, make it something light.

Avoid concentrated fruit juices which normally have hidden sugar. Caffeine may provide instant stimulus to the mind but it can lead to dependency every time you feel you need a boost of energy. Be very wary. Any substance which you depend on can slowly get out of control. And forget a chocolate bar to give you a quick energy boost before a workout. Your meal the previous evening will provide you with all the power you need, not something you eat just beforehand. However, if you feel weak and your stomach won't stop rumbling before the workout, try having an apple or an orange. As for all those body fluid replacement drinks, give them a definite miss. There's only one thing worth sipping during a training session, and drinking after one, and that's water. If you are worried about your blood sugar level, eat more citrus fruits, like grapefruit and oranges, and pineapples.

LOSING WEIGHT

If you are serious about losing weight, you need to make gradual changes to your life in order to tackle the problem, and this means a combination of food and exercise. On the food side, you need to cut out junk food; buy fruit and vegetables instead. These contain large amounts of fibre which will make you feel satisfyingly full without giving you extra calories. Eat less fat as too much fat can lead to health problems, such as clogged arteries, as well as weight problems.

There is no big secret about how to lose the extra weight, you simply burn off more calories than you consume. That's the easy part, knowing *what* to do. The hard part is finding the self-control to do it. Different methods work for different people. One of the best I know was a woman who had put on a lot of weight after the birth of her baby. She was determined to get back in shape and was working out most days, but every now and then she'd go on an eating binge. So one day she brought downstairs a pair of Levi 501s which she hadn't worn for a couple of years and she hung them from the ceiling in the middle of the kitchen. Well, the first three weeks didn't see any increase in weight, but no loss either. However, after eight weeks she had lost ten pounds and was able to get into her favourite jeans again! I'm not saying you have to get out your favourite clothes and hang them all over the kitchen, but you do need to find something that inspires you to keep your self-control, because basically that's all there is to dieting.

I don't believe you should deny yourself something you enjoy eating, as long as it isn't eaten in excess. Obviously you have to be sensible. Cut down gradually on the high-fat, high-sugar foods and try and make them a special treat. That's much more realistic than cutting out all the bad food straight away. For instance, if you like biscuits, try cutting down on how many you eat in a day or a week rather than trying to cut them out altogether. We all have certain weaknesses when it comes to food and eating; mine happens to be ice cream. Once a month I get a video out and relax after dinner with brown bread ice cream!

Changing your eating habits is a mental process as well. If you are feeling low or unhappy, a quick snack, or something sweet, can make you feel better temporarily, but I mean temporarily. After you've eaten the thing you craved, you experience a high but as soon as you've cleared the taste from your mouth you are right back where you started, only now you feel even lower because you ate something fattening. Unfortunately, when you're emotionally upset you never run to the fruit bowl for an orange or an apple, you always find sweets or a chocolate bar to cheer you up. If this only happens occasionally, there's no real harm, but comfort eating continuously can lead to serious weight problems and sometimes needs specialist medical help.

It may help you to write down what you eat in a day and, alongside, how you felt that particular day, then you can compare a good week with a stressful one. Somewhere in between you should find the basis from which to start adapting your food intake. The important thing is to take your time and not to expect a dramatic weight loss quickly. Don't weigh yourself every week, you'll just be discouraged if you haven't lost weight. Wait until you've been following the programme for a few weeks. If the training and the change of diet have been going well there's no need to put yourself under unnecessary pressure by constantly checking to see if anything has happened. If you've been overweight for a year or more or if you are trying to lose seven or eight pounds, you've got to be patient. Think long-term instead of short-term. Everytime you feel like a cream cake or something equally fattening, try to be strong and remind yourself of exactly how you want to look and feel in a few months. Give yourself time, and you'll give yourself the body you want.

It really helps to plan your eating time in the early days, set times do help to stop you snacking in between meals. Coupled with some exercise, you should soon start seeing changes in your body and start feeling better about yourself.

SUMMONING INNER STRENGTH

Remember that none of us feel good about ourselves one hundred per cent of the time. So what happens when you feel low? It may be sparked off by anything – pressure of work, moving house, or a bill you can't pay. Can you summon the inner strength to prevent yourself rushing to the biscuit tin? Well, at the beginning of your training programme I would say no, but once you've been exercising for three or four weeks you've already done the hard graft, so why let yourself down? Your energy levels are up, your mind is more alert, but you feel insecure and fear a snack food attack is getting near, go to the mirror, strip down and take a look at what you've achieved with all your hard work, and ask yourself, 'Do I really want to lose this?' Obviously you can't do this if you're sitting in an open plan office. If your stomach isn't rumbling and it's tension that's making you feel as if you were hungry, try to go for a short walk in the office to stretch your legs. If you are still determined to eat something, eat some fruit. It's a good idea to keep some fresh or dried fruit on your desk. Just the sensation of chewing is often enough to act as a stress reliever.

TIME OF DAY

The time of day you eat is important. Because I'm fussy about my food and dedicated to my training. I never eat at home after eight o'clock in the evening. I start work very early in the morning and if I'm not working I'm training. There's nothing worse than asking your body to perform when you have a semi-bloated stomach, and besides, any fat you consume will stay in your system for longer if you eat late. Remember after a relaxed evening meal you don't feel like going training, it's normally home to bed. If you can only eat in the evening, or you have a lot of social engagements that involve eating late, have a slightly larger lunch than normal and eat a small meal in the evening. Eating a big lunch and avoiding heavy foods in the evening will help you sleep better and avoid getting that very uncomfortable bloated feeling.

20/20 EATING IDEAS

The main thing is to enjoy your food just as you should enjoy your training. If you're not enjoying it, don't do it. Nothing else can really inspire you more than a feeling of well-being. I'm always reminding the people I train of the days when they ate badly, couldn't do stomach exercises properly, ran out of energy early on in the session, or thought they could never feel fit and healthy ever again.

The following are 20 ideas for breakfasts, 20 lunches and 20 dinners, the choice is yours. You can decide what you want to eat and when.

20/20 BREAKFAST IDEAS

1. A selection of mixed dried fruits with freshly squeezed orange juice

2. Almonds, grapes, sliced banana and raisins topped with low fat natural yoghurt

3. Toasted brown bread thinly spread with either jam or peanut butter

4. Scrambled egg on brown toast

5. Porridge with honey and sultanas

6. Raisin and bran muffin

7. Poached egg on brown toast

8. Low fat natural yoghurt with chopped apple, grapes, strawberries and sliced banana

9. Oat bran and raisins with skimmed milk

10. Grilled mushrooms on brown toast

11. Cottage cheese with crispbreads

12. Baked beans on toast

13. Sliced pineapple and pear, mixed with sultanas and topped with low fat natural yoghurt

14. Sugar-free muesli with skimmed milk

15. Granary bread, toasted, topped with a sliced tomato and cottage cheese

16. Grilled kippers with tomato and mushrooms

17. A selection of dried fruits (e.g. apricots, prunes and figs) soaked overnight and served with low fat natural yoghurt

18. Porridge with raisins and almonds

19. Boiled egg with crispbreads

20. Wholemeal fruit scones

Try not to drink tea and coffee, have fresh fruit juices, mineral water or herbal teas instead.

20/20 LUNCH IDEAS

1. Tuna in brine and kidney bean salad (mix the kidney beans with chopped lettuce, spring onions, parsley and tomatoes)

2. Lentil soup with toasted granary bread

3. Baked potato topped with cottage cheese and chives

4. Wholewheat pasta with tomato sauce

5. Grilled trout served with a selection of vegetables (e.g. spinach, boiled potatoes and mushrooms)

6. Brown rice salad with prawns

THE 20/20 EATING PLAN

7. Chicken sandwich with lettuce and tomato made with wholemeal bread

8. Minestrone soup with wholemeal bread

9. Baked potato with baked beans

10. Cottage cheese with carrot and pine nut salad

11. Muesli mixed with banana, pineapple, pear, grapes and greek yoghurt

12. Grilled plaice served with baked potato and mixed salad

13. Onion soup with wholemeal toast

14. Stir-fried vegetables (e.g. broccoli, mushrooms, spring onions and parsley) with prawns

15. Spaghetti in tomato sauce with clams

16. Sweetcorn and tuna salad (combine the main ingredients with unsalted cashew nuts, peas, carrots and tomatoes)

17. Vegetable soup with wholemeal toast

18. Stir-fried prawns with bean sprouts, garlic, spring onions, spinach and mushrooms

19. Grilled chicken breast with baked potato and sweetcorn

20. Grilled halibut with red cabbage, courgettes and boiled parsnips

20/20 IDEAS FOR DINNER

1. Grilled salmon steak served with steamed vegetables

2. Chicken with boiled potatoes, broccoli, green beans and carrots

3. Baked potato with spinach and sweetcorn

4. Poached halibut with herb sauce and salad

5. Curried chicken served with brown rice and mushrooms

6. Spaghetti with tuna and sweetcorn sauce

7. Cannelloni with cottage cheese and spinach served with a green salad

8. Baked potato with butter beans and spinach

9. Fettucine with vegetables (e.g. sweetcorn, asparagus and french beans) in a tomato sauce

10. Turkey casserole with brown rice and vegetables

11. Leek and onion soup with toasted wholemeal bread

12. *Stir-fried chicken with chinese leaves, straw mushrooms and water chestnuts*

13. *Grilled chicken breast served with a baked potato and green beans*

14. *Grilled plaice with kidney beans and mixed salad*

15. *Corn on the cob followed by chicken risotto*

16. *Wholewheat pasta with tomato sauce and mussels*

17. *Vegetarian lasagne with green salad*

18. *Mixed vegetable soup with noodles*

19. *Grilled mackerel served with brown rice, grilled tomato and steamed sliced mushrooms*

20. *Vegetable bake with tomato sauce*

If you need to eat something after your main meal then have a piece of fresh fruit. Accompany your meal with mineral water, or fruit juice, or a combination of both.

ACKNOWLEDGEMENTS

There are various technical people behind the scenes who worked on this and are too numerous to mention, but thank you anyway.

My thanks go to Grahame Dudley, Shona Wood, Felicity Jackson, Kari Tveite and Lene Langgaard for their time, patience and professionalism.

I would also like to thank those who were in this at the beginning but never quite made it to the end: Kay Scorah, Amanda Jones, Anita Hamilton and Barbara Allen.

I would like to thank my brothers, Joe and Lindley, and my sister, Jennifer.

Special thanks to Geoff Howard-Spink for his inspiration over the years and Vivian Grisogono.

Extra special thanks to Cindy Richards for keeping me on track and to Hilary Arnold for instigating the whole thing and having faith in me.